MURDER

25

Editor: Bill Buford
Assistant Editor: Richard Rayner
Commissioning Editor: Lucretia Stewart
Managing Editor: Angus MacKinnon
Associate Publisher: Piers Spence
US Associate Publisher: Anne Kinard
US Advertising: Catherine Tice
Financial Manager: Monica McStay
Assistant to the Editor: Jean Marray
Publishing Assistant: Christina Frank
UK Subscriptions: Gillian Kemp
UK Advertising and Marketing: Alison Ormerod
Editorial Assistants: Tania Rice, Alicja Kobiernicka
Contributing Editor: Todd McEwen
Photo Consultant: Alice Rose George
Picture Research: Lynda Marshall
Design: Chris Hyde
Executive Editor: Pete de Bolla

Editorial and Subscription Correspondence in the United States and Canada: Anne Kinard, Granta, 250 West 57th Street, Suite 1316, New York, NY 10107.

All manuscripts are welcome but must be accompanied by a stamped, self-addressed envelope or they cannot be returned.

Granta, ISSN 0017-3231 is published quarterly for $28 by Granta U.S.A. Ltd, a Delaware corporation. Second class postage paid at New York, NY and at additional mailing offices. POSTMASTER: send address changes to GRANTA, P.O. Box 909, Farmingdale, NY 11737.

Granta is photoset by Hobson Street Studio Ltd, Cambridge, England, and printed in the United States of America by Semline Book Group, Brattleboro, Vermont.

Granta is available on microfilm and microfiche through UMI, 300 North Zeeb Road, Ann Arbor, MI 48106-1346, USA.

Granta is published by Granta U.S.A. Ltd and distributed by Viking Penguin Inc., 40 West 23rd St, New York, New York, USA; Penguin Books Australia Ltd, Ringwood, Victoria, Australia; Penguin Books Canada Ltd, 2801 John Street, Markham, Ontario, Canada L3R 1B4; Penguin Books (NZ) Ltd, 182–90 Wairau Road, Auckland 10, New Zealand. This selection copyright © 1988 by Granta Publications Ltd.

Cover by The Senate. Cover photograph by Michael Trevillion.

Granta 25, Autumn 1988

ISBN 014-00-8608-0

CONTENTS

Ian Jack Gibraltar   13

Martin Amis The Murderee   87

Todd McEwen Drinking Men   129

Graham Smith The Pub   137

Raymond Carver Friendship   155

    What the Doctor Said   162

Tess Gallagher Raymond Carver, 1938 to 1988   163

Nik Cohn Delinquent in Derry   169

Angela Carter 'Tis Pity She's a Whore   179

Don DeLillo The Ivory Acrobat   199

John Berger Means of Transport   213

John Sturrock Muirhouse   229

Notes from Abroad

Amitav Ghosh Tibetan Dinner   250

Notes on Contributors   255

"Damn it, Harper's, I love you—you cruel, beautiful magazine you."

— J.A. Richards, Ottawa, Canada

What? A love letter to a magazine? You bet! Because Harper's is a lot more than just a magazine. Like love, it's a jolt of recognition...a clearinghouse of ideas...a delicious romp through life's more relevant questions.

"The last issue of Harper's left me green with envy of its varied creativity, angry that sloth has kept me from reading it cover to cover, and lusting for the next one."
— Robert B. Lane, Montgomery, AL

You see, unlike other magazines, Harper's Magazine appeals to your emotions, your intellect, your curiosity, and your sense of humor, while it helps you make sense of the world.

"I have been pleased, excited, inspired, thrilled, titillated, touched, convinced, informed, infuriated, and impassioned by each issue of Harper's without exception. I devour each month's panoply of marvels and wait anxiously, breathless for the appearance of the following month's offerings." — Martin F. Katz, Paris, France

There's no telling how you'll react after becoming a subscriber to Harper's Magazine. But it's almost certain your life will change. You'll have more raw data with which to reach your own decisions on important issues. You'll develop a clearer perspective of the world. You'll become reacquainted with eloquence. And you may even fall in love.

"The art of magazine publishing has, indeed, been raised to a new and magical level." — Stephen Garey, Santa Monica, CA

Why not see what magic Harper's Magazine can bring into your life? This gutsy magazine may well be the breath of fresh air you've been looking for.

Yes! I want to add the magic of Harper's Magazine to my life. Please send me a one year's subscription (12 riveting issues) for just $14. That's a savings of 22% off the basic subscription rate and a 42% savings off the regular newsstand price.

I know a good thing when I see it. I prefer a 2-year subscription for $28 — a savings of 42% off the newsstand price.

○ Payment enclosed   ○ Bill me

NAME

ADDRESS

CITY   STATE   ZIP

Canada $21 (CON funds). All other countries $17 (US dollars only). Please allow 6-8 weeks for your first issue. Subscription Dept., P.O. Box 1937, Marion OH 43305

DA91-2

[People, politics, and other passions]

We're talking about the likes of Maxine Hong Kingston, Richard Rodriguez, Lynda Barry, Bobbie Ann Mason, Isabel Allende, Randy Shilts, John Sayles, Kurt Vonnegut. What to learn, how to earn, where to go, what to do, to whom, for whom, and why. Just in time, too. Because all kinds of surprises are on the horizon. Events and ideas that will enlarge your life and change your world. If you give them a chance. If you just say yes.

The all-new Mother Jones. Only seeing is believing.

IAN JACK
GIBRALTAR

L ying half-asleep in my room at the Holiday Inn one night I listened to a song I hadn't heard in twenty years. The tune was 'Marching Through Georgia', but the words did not belong to the American Civil War. I last heard them rising from the crowd at the Glasgow Rangers football ground, where every alternate Saturday the chant is probably bellowed still:

Hello, hello, we are the Billy Boys!
Hello, hello, we *are* the Billy Boys!
We're up to our knees in Fenian blood,
Surrender or you'll die,
For we are the Brigton Billy Boys.

I went to the window. Members of the British popular press were walking unsteadily towards the hotel. Great drinkers and pranksters, these chaps from the tabloids. Already in Gibraltar we'd enjoyed a fortnight of jokes. The first fashion was for water-pistols, which to be strictly accurate was started by the men of Independent Television News (or at least it started at their party, shortly before their guests were thrown into the swimming pool). You might be sitting innocently in a bar or walking down the street when the challenge came from behind, 'Stop, police, hands up!' and you'd turn sharply—very much, I imagine, as Danny McCann and Mairead Farrell turned—and receive a small jet of water straight in the chest. This was the English journalists' reconstruction of the role of the Special Air Service Regiment as executioners of the members of the Irish Republican Army. The role of the Irish Republican Army itself had to wait for the second fashionable joke. A couple of Japanese transmitter-receivers were purchased—the kind of thing strolling British policemen use, the kind of thing we'd been shown in court as an IRA bomb-detonating device—and then demonstrated whenever an evening looked as though it might close unpromisingly in an exchange of civilities. Once, at the Marina, I came across a drunken couple shouting into these machines outside a quayside restaurant. 'Shitbag calling fuckface, shitbag calling fuckface, are you receiving me, over?' 'Fuckface to shitbag, fuckface to shitbag, I am receiving you, over . . .' And now, two weeks into the inquest into the killings of three Irish republicans, this Orange song rolled around the lanes of Gibraltar at one in the morning. 'Hello, hello, we are the Billy Boys . . . up to our knees in Fenian blood.' The only surprise was that Englishmen seemed to know some of the words of a song born of sectarian gang-fighting in Glasgow of the 1930s. But then the English these days are a surprising race.

I write as a Scot, and one with too much of the Protestant in him ever to empathize much with the more recent traditions of Irish republicanism, as well as an ordinary level of human feeling which precludes understanding of the average IRA bomber. But the longer I spent in Gibraltar, the more difficult it became to prop up a shaky old structure—that lingering belief in what must, for lack of a more exact phrase, be called the virtues of Britishness. Both the inquest and its setting played a part in this undermining; perhaps this is what the British government meant when it said that it feared 'the propaganda consequences' of such an inquiry and set up an informal cabinet sub-committee (which included Mrs Thatcher) to combat the eventuality. As it turned out—and who knows what part the informal committee played—the government need not have worried. They got the verdict they wanted, the great mass of British public opinion applauded it and the proceedings were minimally covered in the only foreign media which matter to Britain, which lie in New York and Washington. The government then pressed ahead with 'the war to defeat the terrorist' by banning IRA spokesmen and their political sympathizers from radio and television, where in any case they had scarcely ever appeared, and renewed attacks on the television programme that had ventured to suggest that the Gibraltar killings raised questions which needed proper investigation.

And that, so far as the British government was concerned, closed the Gibraltar affair. One or two journalists remained sceptical, but a week after the verdict the topic had vanished even from the letters columns.

WHat is Gibraltar? John D. Stewart, in the only decent book about the place, wrote that

it may symbolize steadfastness to some and arrogance to others, the British bandit or the British policeman, according to the point of view. But the strongest of all the Rock's suggestions . . . is that concept which used to be called Military Glory, and which we have come to reassess as the slaughter of young men for causes vaguely understood and rapidly discredited and cast aside.

Stewart wrote that more than twenty years ago. Since then Northern Ireland and the Falklands War have intervened to recast the military's position in British life, and the disparaging reassessment of 'military glory' which seemed so enduring to Stewart in 1967 has now itself been reassessed. Who, in 1967, had heard of the Special Air Service Regiment? Who could imagine that in less than two decades its initials, SAS, would comprise a 'sexy headline' for the British tabloids (as an SAS officer told the Gibraltar inquest)? And who could foresee that the *Sun*, then a faltering broadsheet of mildly Labourite views, would become the tabloid-in-chief and cheer-leader of a born-again chauvinism for twelve million readers? Its front-page headlines are inimitable. Of the IRA in general: 'STRING 'EM UP!' Of the three who were shot in Gibraltar: 'WHY THE DOGS HAD TO DIE.' Then again, who in 1967 worried about the fate of Northern Ireland other than the Northern Irish, or about the gerrymandering and discrimination against its minority which kept the province intact? Or who could imagine an ensuing twenty years of terror and counter-terror which, at its last great manifestation on the British mainland, nearly killed a British prime minister and many of her cabinet?

I don't want to go back further. Let's avoid Oliver Cromwell and the potato blight. But is there anything which the head—rather than the gut—can latch on to in this pernicious cycle of cause and effect, some handhold on fairness and reason? One such handhold should be the rule of law, which has always found great favour with the British establishment who speak of it like a sacrament, inviolable, invulnerable to prejudice or political influence: the rule that sets the state morally above those who oppose it by violence. It would follow that the rule of law would be served by truth and that truth—the truthful reconstruction of events—would be the objective of any disinterested and open process of inquiry.

It was the duty of the Gibraltar inquest to use such a process to discover the truth of what happened and thus to see whether that discovery conflicted with the principles of the rule of law—in other words, to establish whether what was true was also legal, whether it was the symbolic British policeman or the symbolic British bandit who shot three unarmed people to death on the streets of Gibraltar on 6 March 1988. It was not a trial, it was an inquest, and was in many people's view a sadly inadequate forum to determine what happened, but the British government insisted that it would be the only one. Six months after the killings, on Tuesday, 6 September, the coroner called his first witness into court. For the next four weeks he heard evidence and argument in a courtroom which, oddly enough, also heard the inquiry into the fate of the crew of the *Marie Celeste* after that abandoned barque was towed to port in Gibraltar in 1872. Sometimes during those four weeks it seemed we were in the presence of a mystery of equal proportions. There was rarely a day when a saying of one of Mrs Thatcher's own party men did not come to mind: in the words of Jonathan Aitken MP, when you try to reconcile effective counter-terrorism with the ancient rule of English law, the result is 'a huge smoke-screen of humbug'.

2

Gibraltar has only one overland entrance and exit. A large lump of Jurassic limestone, it points south into the Mediterranean from Spain. Sea surrounds it on three sides. Only to the north does water give way to land—a flat, low strip of plain about one mile long and half as wide joins Gibraltar to the sweep of the Costa del Sol. The airport runway crosses this strip from east to west, while further to the north are the fences and guard posts which mark the half-mile width of Gibraltar's land frontier. The road into the colony bisects the fences and then the runway. Before visitors can reach the town by road, they must first pass through Spanish and British immigration control and then, if they are unlucky, wait at the traffic lights which control movement across the runway.

Sean Savage, Danny McCann and Mairead Farrell arrived by this route on Sunday, 6 March 1988. Savage came first. He drove a white Renault 5 across the border around 12.30 p.m. and parked it ten minutes later near Ince's Hall at the south end of the town. At 2.30 p.m. McCann and Farrell crossed on foot. By 3.45 p.m. all of them were dead.

It seems likely (no, certain) that we shall never know their exact purpose on that day. None the less, certain aspects of it are beyond dispute. Within hours of their deaths, the Irish Republican Army in Belfast claimed all three as 'volunteers on active service', attached to a unit of the IRA's General Headquarters staff. The next day the IRA admitted that the three had 'access and control over' 140 pounds of explosives. What the IRA would not divulge was the intended target, though on this particular point the British government's scenario has never been seriously challenged. News bulletins on British radio and television on the evening of 6 March quoted briefings in London and Gibraltar which identified not only the target but also the place and time. According to several reports the three dead had intended to blow up the band of the Royal Anglian Regiment, which had recently served in Northern Ireland, as it assembled for the weekly changing of the guard ceremony outside the Gibraltar Governor's residence two days later, on Tuesday, 8 March, at eleven in the morning.

As a description of intention, that may be entirely accurate. It was, however, a minor accuracy embedded in a larger untruth. Throughout Sunday evening and Monday morning the same reports also asserted that a bomb had been found in Gibraltar. The earliest reports were the most circumspect. At 6.25 p.m. on the television news, the BBC's Madrid correspondent said that troops were searching Gibraltar's main street, 'following a report that a bomb had been planted near a public hall . . . but it's not known if that report is genuine.' Three hours later all circumspection was cast aside. At nine o'clock the BBC reported that 500 pounds of explosives had been packed inside a Renault 5 and, according to 'official sources', timed to kill British troops when they assembled for Tuesday's parade. At 9.45 p.m. Independent Television News had further details. Three Irish terrorists had been killed in 'a fierce gun battle'. Their bomb had been defused by 'a controlled explosion'. It was becoming more evident, said ITN's correspondent, 'that the authorities came desperately close to disaster with a bomb being left in a crowded street and a shoot-out when innocent civilians were in the area.'

Monday's newspapers all carried similarly certain accounts, though the size of the bomb varied from 400 to 1,000 pounds. On the BBC's morning radio programme, *Today*, the Minister of State

19

for the Armed Forces, Mr Ian Stewart, again spoke confidently of 'the bomb' and its timing for Tuesday's parade. And yet this bomb was a fiction. There was not and never had been a bomb in Gibraltar, neither had the crowded streets of Gibraltar witnessed a gun battle.

At 3.30 p.m. on Monday afternoon, the Foreign Secretary, Sir Geoffrey Howe, rose to make a statement in the House of Commons. No bomb had been found; neither were the suspected terrorists armed. However, Howe added, 'When challenged they [the dead] made movements which led the military personnel operating in support of the Gibraltar police to conclude that their own lives and the lives of others were under threat. In the light of this response, they were shot.' What Howe then went on to say is worth examination, because its confusing mixture of hypothesis and reality echoed through the Gibraltar affair for the next six months and in fact formed the basis of the British government's case at the inquest:

> The suspect white Renault car was parked in the area in which the band of soldiers would have formed for the Tuesday parade. A school and an old people's home were both close by. Had a bomb exploded in the area, not only the fifty soldiers involved in the parade, but a large number of civilians might well have been killed or injured. It is estimated that casualties could well have run into three figures. There is no doubt whatever that, as a result of yesterday's events, a dreadful terrorist act has been prevented. The three people killed were actively involved in the planning and attempted execution of that act. I am sure the whole House will share with me the sense of relief and satisfaction that it has been averted.

The whole House did, for who would not want to prevent a carnage of innocents? When George Robertson, the Labour opposition spokesman, got to his feet, he seemed oblivious to the fact that the carnage would have been wrought by a bomb which in the course of Howe's speech had quietly ceased to exist. Robertson congratulated the military on their 'well-planned operation':

The very fact that this enormous potential car bomb was placed opposite both an old folk's home and a school underlines the cynical hypocrisy of the IRA . . . This House speaks with one voice in condemning unreservedly those in Ireland who seek to massacre and bomb their way to power. These people are evil. They kill and maim and give no heed to the innocents who get in their way. They must be dealt with, if any democratic answer is to be found.

Consider the statements of both men. Howe admits that there was no bomb; at the same time the shooting of three people prevented 'a dreadful terrorist act' because such an act had been planned in the minds of the dead who at some point in the future would have tried to implement it—had they been alive. This could be read as a confession to a lethal pre-emptive strike. Robertson, in reply, is understandably confused by the semantics of what has gone before. The car bomb seems to him still real and a cause for moral outrage; it is only 'potential' because it has not gone off.

Today it may be easy to separate the various elements in this extraordinary fudge, but at the time the government got away with it, aided by further semantic horseplay from the Ministry of Defence, a credulous media and an impolitic volubility from the IRA. We now know from the bomb disposal officer who gave evidence at the inquest that, if members of the British army in Gibraltar had ever imagined Savage's car to contain a bomb, they knew by 7.30 p.m. on Sunday that it certainly did not. And yet throughout that night and the following morning the Ministry of Defence in London cultivated (or, at the very least, did not correct) the impression that a bomb had been found. At 4.45 p.m. on Sunday the Ministry of Defence confirmed that 'a suspected bomb had been found in Gibraltar.' At 9.00 p.m. a statement was issued to the effect that 'military personnel dealt with a suspect bomb.' The following morning the Ministry was still repeating that 'a suspected bomb had been dealt with.'

There is a strong temptation here, a temptation to use the word 'lie'. Writer (and reader), resist it. According to the Ministry of Defence, the phrase 'suspect bomb' or 'suspect car bomb' is 'a term of art'. As the army's bomb disposal officer explained to the inquest it means no more than a car which, for whatever reason, is thought to contain a bomb. Hence you 'find' a suspect bomb by finding a car and suspecting it. Hence you 'deal with' a suspect bomb either by confirming its presence and defusing or exploding it, or by discovering that no bomb exists. Bomb disposal officers are brave men; nobody need mock the terms of their art. But unfortunately neither the British media nor Mr Ian Stewart, a defence minister, quite grasped the subtleties of their definitions. 'Dealt with' so easily became 'defused', while the size of the notional bomb grew in the minds of reporters in Gibraltar whose only source of information was the gossip of excited Gibraltar policemen. (That night, Ronald Sinden, assistant to the deputy governor, was appointed official press spokesman. He said memorably: 'I am the only source of information, and I have no information.')

These 'facts' had a formidable effect on the IRA, and the two statements it issued tried to correct what were rightly perceived to be untruths. The first did it no harm: 'There could have been no gun-battle because the three volunteers were unarmed.' The second immeasurably helped the British government because, four hours before Howe's statement, the IRA admitted that the three had 'had access and control over' 140 pounds of explosives. This was meant to correct reports of bombs six times that size with the consequent potential carnage, in the belief that the British government or media were simply exaggerating the size of a bomb that had actually been found. But of course, as Howe was to admit, no bomb had been found; the IRA, by misunderstanding the radical nature of the lie it was trying to correct, confessed to a bomb thirty hours before the Spanish police found it forty miles away on the Costa del Sol. From the IRA's point of view, an opportunity to embarrass the British government for thirty hours had been wasted.

Little of this information was ever presented to the inquest as evidence—perhaps rightly; much of it is after and outside the facts. But here, only twenty-four hours after the killings, some lessons can be drawn and kept in mind. One, the British government and its servants are no fools. Two, there are already reasons to distrust the British version of events. And three, London, rather than its colonial outpost, Gibraltar, pulls the strings.

3

One day in Gibraltar I tried to buy a map. This was in early May, a couple of months after the killings. Maps are not hard to come by in Gibraltar, in fact the tourist office gives them away, and these are perfectly good if you want to find your way to the feeding grounds of Gibraltar's famous apes, or the Holiday Inn, or any of the bits and pieces of old military science—steam-driven artillery, stout fortifications, labyrinthine tunnels—which are Gibraltar's chief contribution to history. These maps specialize in the past. About the present they are more reticent. Naturally, I didn't expect them to fill in the details of the naval base or the munitions dumps or the copse of radar and radio masts stuck high on the rock above the town; these are contemporary military secrets. But even with ordinary civilian geography they were vague, as though when it came to housing estates and dual carriageways the cartographer had unhooked his jacket from the back of the chair and taken the rest of the day off.

Farrell, Savage and McCann died in the middle of the civilian quarter. Without a good map it was difficult to follow the arguments about who saw them die, from where. I asked a woman in Gibraltar's bookshop about ordnance survey maps: 'They are not available to the public.' Not knowing Gibraltar, I found this hard to believe. Whatever the vices of the British Empire, one of its virtues is the legacy of careful cartography (imperialism needed to be sure of what it owned) still found in the old British capitals of Asia and Africa and even, I am sure, among those forgotten islands— Pitcairn, St Helena and others—which together with Gibraltar, Hong Kong and the Falklands form the rump of the colonial empire.

Eventually somebody suggested the Public Works Department. There I met the chief draughtsman who asked me to choose from a fine selection of maps of different scales. I picked one, and he went off to have it photocopied. Another man approached.

Would this have anything to do with the shootings?

Only indirectly, I said. It was simply a journalistic exercise to show the exact location, and in the interests of accuracy it would be good to work from the best available map.

The man nodded and went away. I heard him making several telephone calls, successively marked by a rising tone of deference. He returned. 'I am sorry but the Attorney-General has refused me permission to sell you a map.'

The Attorney-General himself! This struck me then as the kind of absurd infringement of liberty that might happen in Evelyn Waugh's Africa. But the better I got to know Gibraltar the more typical it seemed. Gibraltarians do not suffer from an over-developed sense of freedom, and this is not just because they are colonials. Their whole identity is antithetical: to be Gibraltarian is *not* to be Spanish; to be free is *not* to be Spanish. Therefore to be free and Gibraltarian is to be British, because Britain is all that stands between them and a successful Spanish reclamation of their rock. Spain is only a mile from the centre of the town, and yet bread is imported from Bristol (it comes frozen, in lorries) and newspapers from London. No Spanish newspapers can be found; nobody in Gibraltar reads *El País*; the local radio and television stations broadcast only in English. And yet Spanish is the first language of the Gibraltarian, who speaks it at home and in the street (and badly only to Spaniards). To judge by their names, many if not most Gibraltarians are as Spanish as any man or woman from Cádiz or Seville. And yet they mock Spain. Echoing the tabloid xenophobia of the mother country ('dago' and 'wop'), they call Spaniards 'slops' and 'sloppies'. Every weekend they drive out to the resorts of the Costa del Sol and then come home to complain. 'Too many slops on the beach today, Conchita.' 'Let's stay on the Rock next weekend, Luís.' Nor do they believe that Spain has changed. To them it will always be Franco's Spain, rich only in cruel policemen and opaque bureaucrats. But surely, I asked a shopkeeper one day, Spain was now prospering, freer, much more democratic? 'Maybe so, but Spaniards don't understand the word freedom like we do. To them it means the freedom to take drugs and screw around, to behave badly, which they couldn't do under Franco. It's not British freedom or democracy like you and I know it.'

Freedom! Democracy! Executive authority in Gibraltar is vested in the Governor, by tradition a retired British military man, who is appointed by the British Foreign and Commonwealth Office 1,200 miles away in London. The Governor represents the Queen and retains direct responsibility for the colony's defence and internal security. A Council of Ministers, drawn from an elected House of Assembly, looks after lesser domestic matters, but even here the Governor is free to poke a finger in: the list of ministers must first be submitted to him for approval, and he can intervene later if he thinks that any of their policies are a threat to the colony's stability.

Few Gibraltarians object to this semi-autocracy. Could a government in distant Madrid deliver more liberty? And in any case to object is to be pro-Spanish, and the colony owes everything, its origins and continued existence, to Britain. Its limited local democracy is a recent invention: not until after World War Two did the civilian population have any say in its colony's affairs. For 200 years its citizens had been there only to serve the British army and navy, who together with the Dutch had seized the fort from Spain in 1704. Nine years later the Treaty of Utrecht ceded it in perpetuity to the conqueror. The local Spanish were expelled and new camp-followers drawn from Malta and Genoa and the Jewry of Morocco. By the nineteenth century, recurrent sieges and the Rock's bold outline, prickling with guns, had found Gibraltar a firm place in the imperial imagination: 'as safe as the Rock of Gibraltar.'

This historic symbolism is still powerful; 'Free since 1713' says the graffiti on Gibraltar's walls, in the same pugnacious red, white and blue as the slogans ('Remember 1690') of Protestant Belfast. But even more potent are the contemporary facts. Today Gibraltar has a civilian population of about 29,000—20,000 Gibraltarians, the rest British or immigrant Moroccan labour—all of whom squeeze into 2.25 square miles of territory, much of it uninhabitably steep (the Rock rises to 1,400 feet), half of it owned by the Ministry of Defence. The Royal Air Force controls the airport and the Royal Navy the harbour while the army spreads out in barracks to the south. Regiments come here after tours of duty in Northern Ireland, in part for rest and relaxation but also to keep in shape for further tours: according to reports, one of the Rock's large caverns

25

contains a mock Ulster village made of wood—a main street, four side-streets, two shops, a Roman Catholic church called St Malachy's, a school and a women's lavatory. What goes on here under artificial light? Raids, sieges and patrols, one assumes, stun bombs thrown into the ladies' loo, the school stormed, sanctuary denied at St Malachy's.

At night the troops come out to play. The usual sights and sounds of a garrison town: rounds of English lager in the Gibraltar Arms, the Olde Rock and the Angry Friar, chips at Mac's fish bar, maybe a disco down at the RAF base. By eleven the military police are cruising down Main Street. By two in the morning only the brain-dead are left, bumping into shop windows, moaning, crying. "Oo you fackin' callin' a cunt, Kevin? You fackin' cunt you.' Gibraltarians do not complain; these lads are their bread and butter, less an ancestral burden than an heirloom. When the novelist Thackeray visited Gibraltar in 1844 what struck him mainly was the sight of befuddled seamen. But the British Mediterranean fleet was long ago disbanded, and these days respectable young Gibraltarian women no longer weight their handbags with stones. Life in a sense has improved.

This then is the town in which Farrell, Savage and McCann spent the last hour or two of their lives. Had they lived and returned and managed to detonate their bomb, then the result would be what British Intelligence knows as 'a spectacular', worth ten times the publicity of ten bombs in Belfast or County Armagh. As it was, they died among memorials to the enemy's history—Farrell and McCann on the pavement of Winston Churchill Avenue, Savage just below King's Lines—having first been watched from the tombstones of Trafalgar Cemetery, the forecourt of the Anglican Cathedral and a small shop called the Imperial Newsagency where Gibraltar queues up for its air-freighted copies of the *Sun*.

4

Of course they had been watched for months.

According to statements made by the Spanish government

soon after the killings, McCann and Savage were first spotted at
Madrid airport arriving on a flight from Malaga on the Costa del Sol
in November 1987. They were travelling under the aliases Reilly
and Coyne. Around this time the Spanish police also detected a
third IRA member in Malaga, a woman—not Mairead Farrell—
who used the alias Mary Parkin. She, along with Savage and
McCann, returned to the Costa del Sol again in February.

In the meantime the Gibraltar authorities had abruptly
cancelled the changing of the guard ceremony scheduled for
Tuesday, 8 December—the guardhouse, they decided, needed
repainting—and did not resume it until 23 February. It was also on
that day, according to British intelligence, that 'Mary Parkin' once
again visited Gibraltar, to attend the ceremony; she returned the
following Tuesday, 1 March. She then disappeared.

Four days later, on Friday, 4 March, McCann and Savage
reappeared for the third time on the Costa del Sol and were joined
there by a second woman, soon identified as Mairead Farrell. All
three came from Belfast, and exhibits produced during the inquest
(a boarding pass, an air ticket and an airline timetable) suggest that
Farrell took three flights to reach Malaga: from Dublin to Brussels
by Aer Lingus, from Brussels to Madrid by Sabena, and then on to
Malaga by an internal Spanish flight. McCann and Savage may well
have come the same way; the man who drove McCann to Dublin
airport was stopped on his way home to Belfast by British troops at
the border on Thursday evening, 3 March. It seems unlikely that
they would risk travelling on the same series of flights on the same
day—very imprudent terrorist behaviour—but with the question of
the exact sequence of their arrival in Malaga the story reaches
another large contradiction.

Of course they had been watched. Or had they?

In the weeks after the killings, there seemed to be no doubt. On
9 March the Spanish Interior Ministry issued a communiqué which
said that the Spanish police had 'maintained surveillance on the
suspects' until they left Spain and entered Gibraltar. On 21 March
Señor Augustín Valladolid, then the senior spokesman for the
Spanish security services, went further. In a briefing to Harry
Debelius, an American correspondent based in Madrid, Valladolid
said that Spain had accepted a commitment in November to follow
the IRA unit and to keep the British informed of its movements. On

6 March, therefore, Savage, driving a white Renault, was followed all the way down the coast road to Gibraltar. To quote the affidavit later sworn by Debelius, Valladolid said that:

> The method of surveillance used was as follows: (a) four or five police cars 'leap-frogged' each other on the road while trailing the terrorists so as not to arouse suspicion; (b) a helicopter spotted the car during part of the route; (c) the police agents were in constant contact with their headquarters by radio; (d) there was observation by agents at fixed observation points along the road.

Debelius's affidavit also states that Valladolid told him that the Spanish police sent 'minute-by-minute details' of the Renault's movements directly to the British in Gibraltar. Later, in a telephone conversation, Valladolid told him that two members of the British security services had also worked with the Spanish surveillance teams in Malaga.

These statements from members of the Spanish government— and many others—are public knowledge.

But: of course they had *not* been watched.

By the time of the inquest, the matter was no longer certain. There were, of course, no Spanish witnesses—not in a Gibraltar court. And every other witness—members of the Gibraltar police, the British military and British intelligence—flatly denied that the three had been watched. Impossible. Their information, they insisted, was limited to a reported sighting of the three in Malaga.

Of course: otherwise how could the bomb—or the car believed to have contained the bomb—have reached the centre of Gibraltar unchecked?

The likely facts are these: the Spanish police followed McCann and Savage, who were both known to them, but either missed or lost Farrell, whom they had never seen before. All three had aliases and false documentation. Farrell flew out of Dublin as Mary Johnson, but entered Gibraltar as Mrs Katherine Alison Smith, née Harper. For two days the Spanish police could not trace her, though by midday on 5 March they at least knew who to look for. Savage and McCann, on the other hand, presented no difficulty. As Señor Valladolid told Tim McGirk of the *Independent* in May: 'We had complete proof that the two Irishmen were going to plant a bomb. We heard them say so.' Under the names Coyne and Reilly, McCann and Savage checked into the Hotel Escandinavia in Torremolinos, a few miles down the coast from Malaga, towards midnight on 4 March and stayed two nights. Farrell did not register, although some women's clothes were found later in the room: she may have stayed with them, or she may have left her luggage there while she drove through Friday and/or Saturday night to collect and deliver the explosives.

Three cars were hired. A man thought to be Savage using the name John Oakes hired a red Ford Fiesta about midday on Friday, 4 March, from a firm in Torremolinos. Spanish police found the car on Sunday evening, a few hours after the shootings, parked in a car-park several hundred yards from the Gibraltar border. Its contents included false documents, a money belt containing £2,000, a holdall covered in dust and soil which looked as though it might have been buried, several pairs of gloves, a dirty raincoat and anorak, tape, wire, screwdrivers and a small alarm clock. The office manager of the car-hire firm retrieved the car and said it had been driven 1,594 kilometres and was covered in mud. A policeman told him that it had been to Valencia and back.

Using the alias of Brendan Coyne, Savage then hired another car, a white Renault 5, from Avis in Torremolinos about eleven on Saturday morning, 5 March. The next day he drove it into Gibraltar and parked it at Ince's Hall, where the band of the Royal Anglian Regiment would leave their bus, form up and fall out again on Tuesday (during the inquest this became known as 'the de-bussing area'). This car became the suspect car bomb. Some time after the three were shot, an army bomb disposal team blew open its bonnet, boot and doors. It contained car-hire literature.

Farrell also hired a car, the third car, using a British driving licence in the name Katherine Alison Smith, from a firm called Marbessol in Marbella, the next large resort down the coast from Torremolinos. Marbessol's manager recalled that she came into the office about 6.30 p.m. on Saturday evening, 5 March, to make a provisional booking and returned about 10.30 a.m. the next morning to collect a white Ford Fiesta. The manager later told a reporter from Thames Televison, Julian Manyon, that she looked exhausted, 'as though she hadn't been to bed.' Spanish police found the car two days after the killings, on Tuesday evening, 8 March, in an underground car-park just off Marbella's main street and about a hundred yards from the Marbessol office. It had been driven less than ten kilometres. It contained 141 pounds of Semtex, a plastic explosive made in Czechoslovakia, wrapped in twenty-five equal blocks; ten kilos of Kalashnikov ammunition; four electrical detonators made by the Canadian CXA company; several Ever-Ready batteries; and two electronic timing units with circuit boards which, according to the evidence of a Ministry of Defence witness at the inquest, bore the same patterns or 'artwork' as previous IRA bombs. The timers had been set for an elapsed time of ten hours forty-five minutes and eleven hours fifteen minutes: a fail-safe device. If set running at, say, midnight on Monday the first would have detonated the bomb at 10.45 a.m. on Tuesday morning. If it failed, the second timer would give the bomb a second chance half an hour later; which represents the difference in time between the Royal Anglian band leaving the bus and preparing to board again.

Events during those few days in Spain, therefore, may well have unfolded like this: Savage hires the red Fiesta and at some point hands it over to Farrell, whom the Spanish police have the least chance of detecting. Savage then meets McCann and the two idle in Torremolinos while Farrell drives 700 kilometres north to Valencia, collects the explosives, and returns. She may have made this journey on Friday night and Saturday, or just possibly (driving hard) on Saturday night and Sunday morning between her two appearances at the car-hire office in Marbella. Then, either on Saturday around 6 p.m. or Sunday around 10 a.m., she parks the red Fiesta and its bomb in the underground car park. At 10.30 a.m. on Sunday she picks up the white Fiesta, takes it for a run round Marbella's one-way traffic system, then parks it underground next to the red Fiesta. She and one of the men transfer the explosives while the third keeps watch. Savage, whom British intelligence insists was 'the expert bomb-maker', checks that the bomb has been safely transferred and then, at about 11.30 a.m., sets out for Gibraltar in his white Renault 5. Farrell and McCann follow a couple of hours later in the red Fiesta, park it, and cross the border on foot. By this hypothesis, Savage is using the white Renault as—in another of the bomb disposal squad's terms of art—'a blocking-car', a car which would hold the parking space in Gibraltar until the white

Fiesta with the bomb was driven into the same position on Monday night.

Given the traffic in Gibraltar, such a precaution makes sense. To make a small diversion into social history: one consequence of the colony's acute land shortage is that most people live in small apartments; one consequence of its military history is that most apartments are owned by the government. Only six per cent of Gibraltar's homes are owner-occupied. Money can't chase property so it chases cars instead. At the most recent count 8,000 households owned 15,000 cars, or 555 cars for every mile of narrow Gibraltarian road. Parking is a problem which 'Mary Parkin' could not fail to have noticed on her reconnaissance trips.

Very little of this information was mentioned at the inquest.

5

The second time I flew to Gibraltar I noticed a man in Club Class reading Doris Lessing's novel, *The Good Terrorist*. He took it up soon after we lifted from Gatwick and didn't put it down again until we were over the Mediterranean for the Gibraltar approach. This was unusual behaviour. Club seats on Gibraltar flights are taken up mainly by off-shore investors and English expatriates who have 'companies' registered in the colony or real estate on the Costa del Sol. Fugitives from British weather and British tax laws, they tend not to be great readers—books not being duty-free.

The man turned out to be a diplomat with the British Foreign Office. A few months later he returned for the inquest. For four weeks he sat in court with a colleague from the Ministry of Defence and at the end of each day both made themselves available to brief the press; sometimes as the equivalent of 'spin-doctors', there to put the best British gloss on the day's proceedings, and sometimes (helpfully) as translators of military or legal jargon. I can't imagine that Lessing's fictional insights into terrorist behaviour played much of a part here. Her characters are muddled, alienated members of the English middle-class whose violent rage against the state springs from domestic roots, smug parents and unhappy childhoods. They are inept at what they do. Nobody in court suggested that Savage, Farrell and McCann were inept. British military and intelligence witnesses spoke of them as 'ruthless', 'fanatical', 'dedicated', 'experienced' and 'professional'. And yet outside the court, in Gibraltar and London, the government's off-the-record conversations stressed their surprising amateurishness. The British had expected professionalism and planned accordingly (so this private argument ran), only to find themselves up against three people who behaved like novices. Had they behaved like professionals—that is, as the British said they expected them to—then their deaths would not have been controversial. Their amateurism had let the British down.

Who were Savage, McCann and Farrell, and how good were they as professional terrorists?

Sean Savage, the unit's technician, was twenty-three and the youngest and least known. He grew up in Catholic West Belfast. When he was four, the houses on the streets around his birthplace were burned down by Protestant mobs. At the age of seventeen, he joined the IRA; according to his obituary in Ireland's *Republican News*, he was 'a quiet and single-minded individual who neither drank nor smoked and rarely socialized,' and who had 'an extremely high sense of personal security.' Savage seems never to have worked, at least outside his business for the IRA, but unusually for West Belfast both his parents have jobs. His family insist that they knew nothing of his involvement with the IRA, though he was arrested (and then released without charge) in 1982. The parents are by all accounts respectable, religious people. His sister Mary engraves crystal in a Belfast factory. According to her, Savage was an enthusiastic cyclist, amateur cook, Gaelic speaker and night-school student of French. He did well at school. His brother has Down's Syndrome and Savage often took care of him. His obituary records: 'His dedication to the struggle was total and unswerving. To his fellow volunteers he was a strong, steadfast comrade, whose sharp and incisive judgement was relied on in tricky situations.'

Daniel McCann, the unit's leader, was thirty and well known to all sides in the Irish conflict. The *Republican News* spoke of him as 'the epitome of Irish republicanism'. He was first arrested as a sixteen-year-old schoolboy and sentenced to six months imprisonment for rioting. He joined the IRA soon after. Between 1979 and 1982 he spent three terms in prison on charges which included possession of a detonator and weapon. Later in 1982 he was arrested and held with Savage and two others after information was passed to the Royal Ulster Constabulary from a man already in their custody. But the charge was dropped and the four released. His family have run a butcher's shop in the Falls Road, West Belfast's main street, since 1905. At the inquest an SAS officer called him 'the ruthless Mr McCann'. His obituary records: 'He knew no compromise and was to die as he had lived, in implacable opposition to Britain's criminal presence in our land.'

Mairead Farrell had become an important public figure in the armed republican movement by the time of her death, aged thirty-one—and perhaps its most important woman. She joined the IRA aged eighteen and went to jail a year later, in 1976, for planting a bomb at the Conway Hotel, Belfast. Of her two male companions on that bombing, one was shot dead by the RUC on the spot and the other died on a prison hunger-strike in 1981. Farrell served ten years in Armagh jail and Maghaberry women's prison and herself became prominent as a hunger-striker, the 'Officer Commanding' other IRA women prisoners and leader of the 'Dirty Protest', smearing excrement on the walls of her cell. After her release in 1986 she spoke at political meetings throughout Ireland and enrolled as a politics undergraduate at Queen's University, Belfast. She defined herself as a socialist; many also saw her as a feminist. Her family are shopkeepers, prosperous by the standards of West Belfast (they own their own house). Neither her parents nor her five brothers have any affiliations with the IRA. Her four brothers are businessmen; a fifth, Niall, is a freelance journalist and activist for the Irish Communist Party, which sets itself apart from the IRA's 'armed struggle'. In a sense Farrell wrote her own obituary in one of her last interviews: 'You have to be realistic. You realize that ultimately you're either going to be dead or end up in jail. It's either one or the other. You're not going to run forever.'

Mary Savage, Niall Farrell and Seamus Finucan, Mairead Farrell's boyfriend, attended the inquest, and sometimes I'd cross the border to their cheap hotel in Spain and meet them for a meal or a drink. They struck me as intelligent and, I think, honest people; it was often easy to share their indignation at what Niall Farrell described as a 'set-up' or a 'fix'. But our conversation had its limits; discussion of the state's morality could not easily be widened to include the moral behaviour of the deceased. Good terrorists? A case might be made for Farrell. Her only known bombing was preceded by a warning; there were no casualties. As for Savage and McCann, we don't know what part their 'dedication' and 'implacable opposition' played in the ending or maiming of life.

But good terrorists in the professional sense? As Farrell had spent most of her adult life in prison and had been free for only eighteen months, it is difficult to see how she could have perfected her trade. Certainly she was careless or superstitious enough to wear a prison medallion—'Good luck from your comrades in Maghaberry'—around her neck when she entered Gibraltar. McCann? His friends describe him as 'charismatic' and 'a natural leader'. But professional? When he was shot, he was clutching a copy of Flann O'Brien's novel, *The Hard Life*. Farrell's bag contained sixteen photocopied pages of a work entitled *Big Business and the Rise of Hitler* by Henry Ashley Turner Junior.

Both had some of the highest profiles within the IRA. To send either of them on a foreign mission which required safe passage through five different border checks and airport controls sounds like ineptitude. To send both smacks of desperation. Soon after their deaths recriminations began to be heard inside the IRA to this effect. But that was in private.

6

The three bodies stayed in Gibraltar for more than a week. First came the autopsy, then the identification by another Farrell brother, Terence, and a representative from Sinn Fein. The embalming posed a problem. Lionel Codali, the undertaker, said that with few staff members at his disposal the process of restoration and preservation would take at least two days. (In Savage's case, though Codali did not say this, there was a great deal to restore.) Eventually they were ready to be air-freighted. But by whom?

Scheduled flights from Gibraltar go only to London; rumours suggested that baggage handlers at both ends, Gibraltar and Gatwick, might refuse to touch the coffins. Irish charter companies excused themselves on grounds of lack of aircraft. At length an English company took the contract. The bodies were loaded by British servicemen from the Royal Air Force and reached Dublin on Tuesday, 15 March.

They were driven north the same evening. Sympathetic republican crowds turned out to see the cortège as it passed through the counties of Dublin, Meath and Louth, but later, over the border, it was stoned by knots of Protestants from the edge of the motorway. That night at a requiem mass for Farrell in Belfast, Father Raymond Murray said that she had died 'a violent death like Jesus . . . she was barbarously assassinated by a gunman as she walked in public on a sunny Sunday afternoon.' On Wednesday, 16 March, several thousand spectators and mourners turned out for the funeral at Milltown Cemetery, Belfast, where the three were to be buried in the corner of the ground reserved for republican martyrs. About 1.15 p.m., as the first coffin was about to be lowered into its grave, a man began to lob grenades and fire a pistol into the crowd. Mourners chased him from the cemetery and on to the motorway nearby. Often he turned to fire at his pursuers, crying: 'Come on, you Fenian fuckers,' and 'Have some of this, you IRA bastards.' A mourner told *The Times*: 'He seemed to be enjoying it. He was taking careful aim and firing at us, just as if he was shooting clay pigeons.' After the crowd caught up with him, he was beaten unconscious and would have been beaten to death had not the police intervened to carry him away. Three men died during the grenade attack; another two people were critically wounded; sixty-six were hurt.

On Saturday, 19 March, another large crowd assembled at Milltown Cemetery to witness the funeral of Kevin Brady, an IRA activist and one of the three killed in the cemetery three days earlier. As the cortège made its way up the Falls Road a Volkswagen Passat drove towards it, stopped, reversed and then got hemmed in by taxis accompanying the funeral. The car contained two British soldiers in civilian clothes, Corporals Derek Wood and David Howes of the Royal Corps of Signals, who were dragged from the car, beaten, stripped and shot dead, amid shouts of 'We have got two Brits.' Spokesmen for the British army said they could think of no reason why Wood and Howes had driven to the funeral, other than misplaced curiosity. Mrs Thatcher described their deaths as, 'an act of appalling savagery . . . there seems to be no depths to which these people will not sink.'

A lethal chain of events which began in Gibraltar on 6 March had ended thirteen days later in Belfast with a total of eight dead and sixty-eight hurt. The last two deaths, however, imprinted themselves on the British imagination in a way the first six never could. They were young British soldiers killed in view of press and television cameras; the most enduring image from that time shows one of their naked carcasses full-length on the ground like something from an abattoir, with a kneeling priest administering the last rites.

It was not a time that encouraged the asking of difficult questions about the killings in Gibraltar. None the less, by the end of the month, Amnesty International announced that it intended to investigate the shootings to establish whether they were 'extrajudicial executions'. The government was contemptuous. Mrs Thatcher told the House of Commons: 'I hope Amnesty has some concern for the more than 2,000 people murdered by the IRA since 1969.' One of her former ministers, Ian Gow, described the investigation as 'a stunt . . . undertaken apparently on the behalf of three terrorists mercifully now dead.' But real government fury had yet to show itself.

The British press had stayed obediently, perhaps slothfully, silent on Gibraltar—this was not one of its more glorious moments. Then in late April Thames Television announced that its current affairs team had made a thirty-minute documentary on the shootings which included eyewitness accounts of how the three had died. The government moved quickly to have it stopped. Sir Geoffrey Howe telephoned the chairman of the Independent Broadcasting Authority to ask him to postpone the programme's transmission until after the inquest. It was the job of the law rather than 'investigative journalism' to throw light on the Gibraltar affair: journalism would simply muddle or prejudice the legal process. We should await a legal verdict, even though Sir Geoffrey Howe himself had not obeyed that stricture when on 7 March he issued his version of events, which had, by its amplification in the press, become the conventional British wisdom.

When the Independent Broadcasting Association resisted Sir

Geoffrey, Tom King, the Northern Ireland Secretary, told Parliament that the programme amounted to 'trial by television'. Mrs Thatcher took up the phrase. 'Trial by television or guilt by accusation is the day that freedom dies,' she told a group of Japanese journalists on the day before the broadcast. When asked if she was furious, as she often is, she replied that her reaction went 'deeper than that'.

The programme, 'Death on the Rock', went out on the evening of 28 April. The response was immediate: an immense uproar, which increased when the BBC, also refusing to bow to government pressure, broadcast a similar investigation a week later in Northern Ireland. Both programmes implied that the government's version of events, as stated by Sir Geoffrey Howe to Parliament on 7 March, was not necessarily complete. Thames Television had found witnesses who said that they had heard no warning before the shots were fired, that McCann and Farrell had their hands up in surrender when they were killed, and that two and possibly all three of them seemed to have been shot again after they fell to the ground. The programme had discovered these witnesses by knocking on the doors of the apartments surrounding the Shell petrol station on Winston Churchill Avenue, the scene of the killings. It is a traditional journalistic method of investigation. It is also a traditional police method, but not one, at that stage, that had been adopted by the Gibraltar constabulary. Several dozen apartments had a good view of the spot where Farrell and McCann died. The programme's researcher, Alison Cahn, found that most of their occupants were reluctant to discuss what, if anything, they had seen on 6 March. Two did, however.

Mrs Josie Celecia said that she was looking from the window of her flat, which faces the petrol station from the other side of Winston Churchill Avenue, when she heard two shots. She turned to look in their direction and then heard four or five more shots as a casually dressed man stood over two bodies.

Mrs Carmen Proetta, whose flat lies 100 yards to the south of the Shell station on the same side of the road, gave a more complete, and even more controversial, picture. She had been at her kitchen window when a siren sounded and several men with guns jumped over the barrier in the middle of Winston Churchill Avenue, and rushed towards a couple who were walking on the pavement near the petrol station. 'They put their hands up when they saw these men with the guns in their hands. There was no interchange of words, there were just shots. And once they [the couple] dropped down, one of the men, this man who still had the gun in his hand, carried on shooting. He bent down and carried on shooting at their heads.'

A third witness, Stephen Bullock, described what he had seen about 150 yards to the south. Bullock, a lawyer, had been walking with his wife and small child when he heard a siren and shots almost simultaneously. He looked in the direction of the sounds, towards the petrol station, and saw a man falling backwards with his hands at shoulder height. 'He was still being shot as he went down.' The gunman was about four feet away. 'I think with one step he could have actually touched the person he was shooting.'

Other evidence from two anonymous witnesses said that Savage had also been shot on the ground, while a retired bomb and ballistics expert with a distinguished army record in Northern Ireland appeared on the programme casting doubt on the possibility that anyone could have believed that Savage's white Renault 5 contained a bomb. According to this expert, George Stiles, it would be obvious to any experienced observer that the Renault was not low enough on its springs—the wheels were not against the wheel-casings—and that therefore the car 'clearly carried no significant weight of explosives.'

The response of the press was curious. Little of its coverage addressed the programme's new evidence. Instead a campaign was begun to discredit the witnesses and the journalists at Thames Television. Two of the government's strongest media supporters—Rupert Murdoch's *Sun* and *Sunday Times*—led the campaign, and the viciousness of their attacks surprised even some of the newspapers' employees. Mrs Carmen Proetta in particular took a mauling. She emerged on the front page of the *Sun* as an anti-British whore ('THE TART OF GIB'), an allegation which had its perilous foundation in the fact that her name had briefly appeared on company documents as a director of a Spanish tourist and escort agency.

The programme emerged as such a powerful challenge to the government and its version of events that the government has not, apparently, forgiven Thames Television. But at the time, the government's complaints wore a nobler face: journalism had no place in the legal process, and that process, as it had said many times before, was entirely a matter for the Gibraltar coroner and magistrate, Mr Felix Pizzarello.

But what had happened to that process? There was still no date fixed for the inquest. Two months went by before the coroner's office finally announced that the inquest would begin on 27 June. For a fortnight or so, this date held good. Then at 11 a.m. on Monday, 27 May, a press spokesman for the prime minister's office announced that the inquest would be indefinitely postponed. The government, said the spokesman, had received this news from Mr Pizzarello over the weekend, adding that the postponement was of course entirely Mr Pizzarello's decision. The government could not interfere with Mr Pizzarello's timetable.

The spokesman, however, was unaware that Pizzarello himself did not know of the decision he had taken. The same morning that the government announced the decision made by Pizzarello over the weekend, Pizzarello was telling Dominic Searle, a reporter on the *Gibraltar Chronicle* and correspondent for the Press Association, that he was considering a postponement—but only considering it. When Searle heard the news from London he went back to the coroner's office, to be told that Pizzarello was still only considering a postponement. Eventually, at 4 p.m., the coroner vindicated Downing Street's prescience and announced an indefinite postponement.

There is a temptation here, a temptation to use the word 'horseshit'. Reader, resist it. Pizzarello had good reason to delay proceedings, and the pressure came from below rather than above. Ten days before, a young Gibraltar woman, Miss Suyenne Perez, had written to the coroner in her capacity as chairwoman of the Gibraltar International Festival of Music and the Performing Arts to remind him that this year's festival was scheduled to begin on 24 June. Four days of it would coincide with the inquest. Perhaps, Miss Perez wrote to the coroner, he would like to consider changing his dates to avoid an undue strain on police resources?

In the event, the festival consisted of one beautiful baby contest, and, in the evening, a number of recitals held in the school halls. Neither the British government nor Pizzarello nor the Gibraltar police ever advanced any other reason for the inquest's postponement. And so the inquest was once again delayed, this time for a further two months, by which time Parliament had gone on holiday—there would be no troublesome questions—and Mrs Thatcher could prepare for a visit to Spain.

7

During late summer a peculiarly local climate overcomes Gibraltar. For several weeks life conducts itself under a thick cloud, while only a mile away Spain sparkles in the sun. Gibraltarians make jokes about this cloud—even our weather is English! They know it as 'the Levanter' and its causes are interesting enough. The prevailing wind in Gibraltar is easterly. From June to September it blows across a thousand miles of warm Mediterranean, gathering moisture on the way, until it strikes the rock's sheer eastern face and soars up 1,400 feet. The air cools rapidly, its moisture becomes vapour, and a dense white cloud tumbles over the rock's escarpment to blot out the sun from the town, which lies in a windless pocket to the west. The effect is spectacular—look up from Main Street towards the ridge and you can imagine a blazing, smoking forest on the other side—but also oppressive. As the colony's historian, John D. Stewart, writes:

> It obscures the sun, raises the humidity to an uncomfortable degree, dims and dampens the town and the ardour and enterprise of everyone in it. It is, inevitably, hot weather—too hot—when this added plague arrives, and now it is hot and humid and without even the benefit of brightness.

It was September, the Levanter season, and we had gathered at last for the inquest. Everybody sweated. The courtroom had a high ceiling from which fans had once been suspended; an effective system of Victorian ventilation helped by the windows high in the walls. But as part of some colonial modernization the fans had been removed, the windows double-glazed and air-conditioning installed. The air-conditioning had broken down.

Sometimes the coroner ordered the doors to be opened; papers would then blow around; the doors would be closed again. Upstairs in the press gallery shirts grew dark from sweat stains.

The court was wood-panelled in the English fashion, brown varnish being sober and traditional, and from the gallery its layout looked like this. Straight ahead and raised above the courtroom floor sat the coroner. A large plaster representation of the royal coat of arms was stuck to the wall above him; the lion and the unicorn, splendidly done up in red, white and blue, picked out in gold, and complete with its legends in courtly French which say that the English monarchs have God and right on their side and that evil will come to those who think it.

To the right sat the eleven members of the jury—all from Gibraltar, all men (women must volunteer for jury service but few do). Counsel shared a bench in the well of the court. On the left, Mr Patrick McGrory, the Belfast lawyer who was representing the families of the dead without a fee. In the middle, Mr John Laws, who represented the British government and its servants in Gibraltar. On the right, Mr Michael Hucker, who represented the soldiers of the Special Air Service Regiment.

The purpose of the inquest was to determine, not guilt or innocence, but whether or not the killing was lawful. The government badly needed the jury to return a verdict of lawful killing. The relatives of the deceased sought to demonstrate that the three had been murdered, and, although dealt with fairly by the coroner, they and their counsel always felt that they were at a disadvantage: inquests, unlike trials, do not require the advance disclosure of witnesses' statements, and so McGrory had no idea what most witnesses would say before they said it. As it was the Crown's inquest, the Crown's counsel read the statement of every witness beforehand. Laws, therefore, could think ahead, while McGrory, always struggling to keep up, had no way of testing evidence he was hearing for the first time against what later witnesses might say.

McGrory was at a disadvantage in other respects. John Laws had been provided with 'public interest immunity certificates' which he invoked whenever the line of inquiry looked as though it might risk 'national security'. So, in the public interest, the inquest learned little about the events in Gibraltar, Spain, Britain or

Northern Ireland before 5 March. Nor did it ever discover the true extent of the military and police operation on 6 March, though it clearly involved many more people than appeared in court.

There was some question about who in fact would appear in the first place. Would the SAS testify? Although members of the SAS were servants of the Crown and although the Crown was holding the inquest, the government was, it said, unable to force the soldiers to come to court. Finally—with a curtain round the witness box to protect them from recognition and possible retribution from the IRA—the soldiers, voluntarily, appeared. A total of eighty witnesses passed through the court, but eighteen of them were visible only to the coroner, jury and counsel. These eighteen anonymous witnesses—referred to always by a letter—were drawn from, in addition to the SAS, MI5, Special Branch and the Gibraltar Police.

Soldier A was clearly working-class and from the south of England—perhaps London. This much could be deduced from his accent. He was also the one who fired the first shot—at Danny McCann on Winston Churchill Avenue. Soldier B was standing next to Soldier A, and subordinate to him. Soldier B was the first to shoot Mairead Farrell.

Down the street were Soldiers C and D. They were also working-class but from the north: Soldier C was probably from Lancashire. He was the first one to shoot Sean Savage. Soldier D, his subordinate, then began firing.

Two teams, then: Soldier A and Soldier B, Soldier C and Soldier D. Other teams were on the ground—the inquest heard of soldiers at the airport—but there was no way of knowing their exact number. The two 'known' teams reported to a tactical commander, Officer E, who was in constant touch with them via radio. Officer E reported in turn to Officer F, who was the overall commander of the military operation. Both officers spoke as though they had attended public schools.

Officer F was also assisted by a bomb-disposal expert, an Officer G. This, then, made up the SAS team:

Soldier A: the first to shoot Danny McCann.
Soldier B: the first to shoot Mairead Farrell.
Soldier C: the first to shoot Sean Savage.
Soldier D: Soldier C's subordinate.

Officer E: the tactical commander of the two teams of soldiers.
Officer F: the overall military commander.
Officer G: the bomb-disposal expert.

There was also Mr O, a senior figure in British intelligence whose information instigated the entire operation. But in addition to the SAS there was a large number of 'watchers', in all likelihood drawn from MI5. At the trial their initials were H, I, J, K, L, M, and N. It is probable that there were many more watchers. And finally, although most of the Gibraltar police testified without the curtain, there were three who sheltered behind it: Policeman P, Policeman Q and Policeman R.

The visible witnesses comprised the following: twenty-four members of the the Gibraltar police; twelve experts on pathology and ballistics—seven from the London Metropolitan Police and two from the army; a map-maker from the Gibraltar Public Works Department; and twenty-five people who were, by accident, close to the scene of the killings. But these twenty-five people included five who worked for the Gibraltar Services Police guarding military installations, one who was an off-duty member of the ordinary Gibraltar police, one who was a former Gibraltar policeman, one who worked for the Ministry of Defence, one whose father was in the Gibraltar police, and three who worked for various branches of the Gibraltar government. No more than sixteen witnesses out of seventy-eight, therefore, could be said to be completely independent of either the British government or the administration of its dependent territory.

McGrory also had a problem with money. He had given his services free and had little to spare. The legal authorities in Gibraltar, meanwhile, had decided to charge ten times the usual rate for the court's daily transcripts. Four days before the inquest began they raised the price from 50p to £5 per page—which amounted to between £400 and £500 per day. McGrory couldn't afford it and instead relied on longhand notes made by a barrister colleague from Belfast. McGrory was the only person in court who wanted to ask awkward questions of the official account. But for all these reasons his ability to ask awkward questions was sometimes severely limited.

8

Over the next few weeks I sometimes wondered what Farrell, Savage and McCann made of Gibraltar during their last few hours there. Did they notice, for example, the number of fit young men in sneakers and jeans wandering aimlessly about? Did they realize that few of them were ever far away?

I wonder if they spotted the two young men lounging in the Trafalgar Cemetery. They were Soldier C and Soldier D. They were the two men who would kill Sean Savage. When Farrell looked into the Imperial Newsagency, did she see a man suddenly turn his back? He was Soldier B. Did she glimpse his face, even briefly? He was the man who would kill her. Later, walking down Line Wall Road, looking over her shoulder from time to time (which, we heard, she did frequently), did she think that the two men hurrying behind her were vaguely familiar? They were, once again, Soldiers C and D.

What about Savage? There was the chap who passed him in Lovers' Lane. He was Policeman P of the Gibraltar police. They stared at each other, or, as Policeman P would express it to the court, he and Savage made 'eye-to-eye contact'. Savage had been in town at least ninety minutes longer than the others, doubling back on his tracks, suddenly stopping and watching at the end of alleyways. Around two o'clock, did he see the fellow hanging about outside the Anglican Cathedral? That was Watcher H of MI5, who likewise spent the afternoon doubling back on his tracks, suddenly stopping at the end of alley-ways. According to Watcher H, Savage employed 'very subtle anti-surveillance techniques.' All three, he said, were 'highly alert and sensitive . . . to all the movements and events that were happening around them.'

The authorities in Gibraltar had been waiting for Savage and McCann, if not Farrell, for weeks and possibly months. The source of their information was Mr O, a senior British intelligence officer and specialist in counter-terrorism and the IRA. Mr O told the court that his representative in Gibraltar (who never appeared as a witness) had briefed the governor, the commissioner of police and military officers with details of the IRA's intention: the time and the target, the method (car-bomb), the kind of explosives that would be used (Semtex) and the names of Savage and McCann. When these details were passed on to Gibraltar's commissioner of police, Mr Joseph Luís Canepa, Canepa then requested military assistance; the assistance would turn out to be an unspecified number of troops from the Special Air Service Regiment which specializes in covert anti-terrorist operations—most famously ambushes—in Northern Ireland.

An advisory group was then established, comprising Canepa, two of his most senior policemen, and the principal parties from Britain: Officer G, the bomb-disposal expert; Officer E, the SAS tactical commander; Officer F, the overall military commander; as well as intelligence officers from MI5. Together they devised a strategy that can be summarized as 'arrest, disarm, defuse.' Secrecy was paramount. According to Police Commissioner Canepa, very few members of the Gibraltar police force knew of the operation. A secret operational headquarters was set up (probably in the Governor's Residence on Main Street, though the location was never revealed to the inquest). There, at midnight, between 5 and 6 March, a meeting of police, military and intelligence officers was told that the three suspects were in Spain and that they could be expected to arrive during the next forty-eight hours.

A secret operational order was issued.

Soldiers and police were briefed about how they would put the order into effect. First, the offenders would be arrested, 'using minimum force'; second, they would be disarmed and their bomb defused; then evidence would be gathered for a court trial. SAS soldiers would make the arrests and hand over the suspects to armed Gibraltar policemen.

By this stage, the operation had a code-name, 'Operation Flavius'. The order for Operation Flavius had many appendices, the most vital being the rules of engagement. The written instructions that Officer F, the overall military commander, was meant to obey included the following:

USE OF FORCE

You and your men will not use force unless requested to do so by the senior police officer(s) designated by the Gibraltar police commissioner; or unless it is necessary to do so in order to protect life. You and your men are not then to use more force than is necessary in order to protect life . . .

OPENING FIRE
You and your men may only open fire against a person if you or they have reasonable grounds for believing that he/she is currently committing, or is about to commit, an action which is likely to endanger your or their lives, or the life of any person, and if there is no other way to prevent this.

FIRING WITHOUT WARNING
You and your men may fire without a warning if the giving of a warning or any delay in firing could lead to death or injury to you or them or any other person, or if the giving of a warning is clearly impracticable.

WARNING BEFORE FIRING
If the circumstances in [above] paragraph do not apply, a warning is necessary before firing. The warning is to be as clear as possible and is to include a direction to surrender and a clear warning that fire will be opened if the direction is not obeyed.

Those were the rules. Here, once again, are the facts. Farrell, Savage and McCann were unarmed; the car Savage had driven into Gibraltar did not contain a bomb; all three were shot dead. Can the facts be made to square with the rules? Can the facts be reconstructed or revealed in a new light, as it were, which would make their pattern on 6 March conform with the law? The recent history of Northern Ireland supplies an answer.

9

Soldiers of the SAS were first dispatched to Northern Ireland in 1976 by the then Secretary of State for Northern Ireland, Merlyn Rees. This year Rees admitted that their deployment had as much to do with public relations as counter-terrorism: the Labour government needed to be seen to be 'getting on top of terrorism', and the piratical, daredevil reputation of the regiment, familiar only to students of late colonial counter-insurgency (Malaya, Borneo, Aden), might therefore be fostered to appease public concern. 'Who Dares Wins,' says the regimental motto. The SAS could be expected to strike first.

Two years later, on 11 July 1978, an SAS unit shot and killed a sixteen-year-old boy, John Boyle, at a cemetery near his home in County Antrim. The previous day Boyle had discovered an arms cache in the cemetery and told his father, who then informed the Royal Ulster Constabulary. The RUC passed on the information to the army, who then 'staked out' the cemetery with soldiers from the SAS. The next day young Boyle was cutting hay in a field near the cemetery and at about ten in the morning went back to see if the arms were still there. The SAS opened fire. Boyle's father, meanwhile, had been warned by the RUC about the stake-out. He ran to the graveyard to look for his son and was joined by Boyle's elder brother, who had also been haymaking in another field. The SAS arrested both men. The army's press office quickly issued a statement: 'At approximately 10.22 a.m. this morning near Dunloy a uniformed military patrol challenged three men. One man was shot; two men are assisting police enquiries. Weapons and explosives have been recovered.'

The SAS version of events did not please the RUC. The Boyles were a Catholic family and therefore an unusual and prized source of important information. The SAS had now shot one of the family dead. In its press statement, the police denied the army's implication that the Boyles were connected with terrorism, prompting a second army statement confessing to inaccuracies in the first: 'Two soldiers saw a man running into the graveyard. They saw the man reach under a gravestone and straighten up, pointing an Armalite rifle in their direction. They fired five rounds at him. The rifle was later found with its magazine fitted and ready to fire.'

There had been no challenge—a warning would have been 'impracticable'.

Eight months later, in the wake of a public outcry caused by the publication of the pathologist's report, two SAS soldiers were charged with murder. Evidence at their trial showed that the rifle had not been loaded, contrary to the army's second statement, and the judge was unable to decide if Boyle had ever picked it up. He concluded that the army had 'gravely mishandled' the operation and that the only SAS soldier to give evidence—one of the two charged—was an 'untrustworthy witness' who gave a 'vague and unsatisfactory' account. The two were found not guilty none the less. Their 'mistaken belief' that they were in danger, said the judge, was enough to acquit them.

Over the past fifteen years many other killings in Northern Ireland have hinged in court on this question of 'mistaken belief' and the subsequent use of 'reasonable force'. Perhaps the most famous is the case of Patrick McLoughlin, who was shot dead with two other unarmed men as they tried to rob a bank in Newry in 1971. McLoughlin's widow, Olive Farrell, sued the Ministry of Defence for damages in the Northern Ireland High Court, but the jury decided that McLoughlin was to blame for his own death. It had been persuaded by the argument that British troops, in a stake-out or ambush similar to the one that killed Boyle, had shot three men because their commanding officer had suspected, 'with reasonable cause' (though wrongly), that the three were trying to plant a bomb which would endanger life. Shooting was the only practicable, and therefore reasonable, means of arrest. As Lord Justice Gibson, the Northern Ireland judge later to be killed by a republican bomb, commented:

> In law you may effect an arrest in the vast extreme by shooting him [the suspect] dead. That's still an arrest. If you watch Wild West films, the posse go ready to shoot their men if need be. If they don't bring them back peaceably they shoot them and in the ultimate result if there isn't any other way open to a man, it's reasonable to do it in the circumstances. Shooting may be justified as a method of arrest.

The case of Farrell *versus* the United Kingdom was appealed unsuccessfully in the House of Lords and went eventually to the European Commission on Human Rights, where the British government settled out of court in 1984 by paying Farrell £37,500. The payment ensured that the commission's ruling remains confidential, though the British government's submission to the commission has been published. Britain argued that the jury in the Farrell case had been directed correctly because it had been told that it would be unreasonable to cause death 'unless it was necessary to do so in order to prevent a crime or effect the arrest;' and that the concepts of 'absolutely necessary' and 'reasonable' were the same thing when it came to killing a person believed to be a terrorist bomber.

'Belief', 'believed', 'reasonable'. The same words appear in Operation Flavius's rules of engagement. The inquest heard them with dripping regularity. Out of the graveyards of Ulster, one may suspect, reasonably, came the bones of the government's legal case in Gibraltar; a case, like Boyle's and McLoughlin's, of mistaken belief.

10

Could there really have been a bomb activated by a button?

In the months preceding the inquest, the *Sunday Times* became essential reading if only because its reports seemed to reflect so reliably the official leaks that served to strengthen the government's original story: that Farrell, McCann and Savage had all made 'suspicious movements'—suspicious enough to justify shooting the three of them: either they were going for guns or they were about to detonate a bomb with a radio-controlled device. That they had neither guns nor radio-controlled devices obviously diminished the credibility of the government's story, which was diminished further following the statements made for the Thames Television programme by bomb expert George Stiles: that he had never known the IRA to explode a radio-controlled bomb without a view of the target, and that it was unlikely in the extreme that the kind of transmitter used by the IRA could have been sophisticated enough to send a signal a mile from the bomb with buildings in between.

Nevertheless, on 8 May, ten days after the programme, the *Sunday Times* supplied an answer of sorts (REVEALED: WHY THE SAS SHOT THE IRA). According to military sources, the SAS had 'secret intelligence which convinced them that the gang was able to detonate a bomb by using a sophisticated remote-control device.' In the event, the inquest heard of no sophisticated remote-control device. But 'sophisticated' was not the keyword in the *Sunday Times* report. The keyword was 'convinced'. In the face of the apparent facts (no bomb, no devices, no gun) and the Thames

Television programme, the government's case rested on the SAS's conviction that McCann, Farrell and Savage *could* have been carrying radio-controlled devices.

At the inquest Mr O, the senior intelligence officer from London, admitted that while so much of his information had been flawless—names, date, times—he had blundered in three respects: first, the three suspects were not, as he had predicted, armed; second, as he had not predicted, they had used a blocking-car; and third 'when the car bomb was eventually discovered in Marbella it did not contain a radio-controlled device, it contained a timer.'

Why had he been so sure about a radio-controlled bomb?

Because Mr O had overrated the morality of the IRA. The bombing at Enniskillen on 8 November 1987 was central to Mr O's thinking: eleven civilians had been killed and fifty wounded at an Armistice Day parade, eliciting so much protest from so many different parts of the Irish community, north and south, that it had shaken the IRA, and the organization had apologized for 'a mistake'. The bomb, it implied, had gone off at the wrong time. Mr O assumed that IRA would not run the same risk of civilian casualties in Gibraltar, and radio-control was the only way to ensure that the bomb was exploded when the bombers were sure it would destroy the intended target—the British troops. It was unlikely, Mr O said in court, that the IRA would use a timing device, 'because, once a timer is started, it is virtually impossible to stop it [unless the bombers] go back to the bomb and actually disarm it, which is a highly dangerous procedure.'

The only fact that Mr O, or anyone else, could summon to support the assumption that there would be a radio-controlled device was in the discovery by Belgian police on 21 January of a car containing a large amount of Semtex, four detonators and 'equipment for a radio detonation system' of a kind familiar in Northern Ireland. For reasons never disclosed, Mr O assumed the Gibraltar bomb would be of a similar type.

McGrory was puzzled by the statement made by Mr O that a radio-controlled bomb would be 'safer' for the terrorists because they could get away. Wouldn't some form of timer be just as safe for them?

'Yes,' said Mr O, 'but if the parade had been cancelled at the last moment because it rained, which we understood was a possibility, there would have been absolutely no way of reversing the bomb. It would have been set and would have exploded willy-nilly, and the people who would have been injured and killed would not have been military personnel.'

Mr O's answer contained a dramatic implication which went unnoticed at the time, because McGrory, imagining that Mr O thought the bombers intended to detonate their radio-controlled device from Spain, went on to ask Mr O if he had ever heard of a case in which the IRA had exploded such a bomb from such a distance, without 'line of sight' of the target. Mr O said he had not; in fact the army never believed that the IRA would detonate its bomb from Spain in the first place. The Army believed it would be detonated in Gibraltar, with a clear view of the target. What would then be the point of radio-control? To avoid civilian casualties the bombers would need to watch the target. They would need to be, as it turned out, high on the Rock to the east of the car-park at Ince's Hall, hemmed in by buildings and walls on its other three sides.

The bomb-disposal expert, Officer G, and his counsel, Michael Hucker, explained:

Michael Hucker: What would the position on the Renault be? The bomb is planted on the Sunday; the terrorists walk north and stay in Spain. One of them comes back on the Tuesday morning at about ten o'clock and goes to the Rock with a pair of binoculars and one of those [indicating a radio transmitter-receiver]. What would he be able to do?

Officer G: He would be able to maximize the effectiveness and the use of his bomb because he could wait until the band was assembled *in toto*, in that nice clear area of the Ince's Hall car-park. He could wait until they had formed up and from the housing estate [up on the Rock] he could then press the transmit button and destroy them all.

This is the terrorists conforming to what might be called the Dr Jekyll hypothesis. This is the terrorists showing a high regard for the sanctity of civilian life by putting their own lives at considerable risk, entering one of the world's most heavily defended and patrolled military outposts—not once, but twice. They leave a car-bomb in an obvious place for two days, risking the chance that it will be detected, defused and the area staked out. And then, assuming that it has not been detected or defused or the area staked out, they rush to reach Gibraltar's only exit, one and a half miles away, before the authorities close the border in the wake of a massive explosion.

But, apart from its improbability, the Dr Jekyll hypothesis contains a serious flaw. If the bombers are prepared to take such care to protect innocent people that they will blow up only a precise military target at only a precise time on a Tuesday afternoon, how are they such a threat to life on the preceding Sunday that they need to be killed? The answer is in the Mr Hyde hypothesis, revealed to the court by Officer F, the SAS military commander of the operation. According to Officer F, it was expected that Farrell, Savage and McCann would carry radio-detonating devices so that, if their operation was 'compromised'—that is, if they thought they were about to be arrested—they would explode the bomb at any time, whatever the consequences to civilian life. In court, McGrory tried to unravel the thinking.

McGrory: Isn't that [the Hyde hypothesis] quite contrary to the other supposition, or deduction, that in fact their anxiety after Enniskillen and all that would be to avoid civilian casualties?

Officer F: Yes, but that's two different deductions. There's one deduction . . . which is that in their terms the perfect operation is where they can use the radio-controlled device in theory to minimize the number of casualties. But the other supposition is that when they are cornered a different set of factors pertain, in my opinion, and when cornered they will have no qualms about either resorting to weapons or pressing a button, knowing that the bomb was there . . . they'd achieve some degree of propaganda success, apart from casualties, of exploding a bomb in the centre of Gibraltar.

McGrory: I'm sorry, I can't follow that, because, if the submission was that Enniskillen caused a propaganda disaster of great magnitude for them, why should they cause another propaganda loss like that, not a propaganda gain that you are talking about?

Officer F: In my opinion, they are adept at turning disaster into triumph in their own propaganda terms, and therefore, if they could claim that they had got a bomb into Gibraltar, that they had . . . successfully exploded it in Gibraltar, I believe that they would claim that to be a propaganda success and would try and derive credit and publicity from it.

McGrory: Propaganda success that had emulated Enniskillen, which was the greatest propaganda disaster? Surely that can't be right?

Officer F: I believe it is.

The jury was being asked to accept that, an hour or so before McCann, Farrell and Savage were killed, the authorities had come to believe the following: that the three would use a car-bomb to be detonated by radio on Tuesday morning; that the car itself was expected to arrive on Monday evening; that a car arrived instead on Sunday which the authorities nevertheless believed to be a car-bomb rather than a blocking-car; that the three bombers would leave and that one (or more) of them would return on Tuesday; that each time the bombers crossed the border and its immigration and customs controls they would be armed and in possession of detonating devices; and that, finally, Savage, using an Irish passport in his known pseudonym of Brendan Coyne, had not been spotted driving the Renault over the border despite the fact that British surveillance teams and the Spanish border police were awaiting his arrival.

This last apparent mistake—the failure to spot Savage as he crossed the border—was crucial to the government's case. Otherwise it would have to explain why it had allowed Savage to drive a car suspected of containing a bomb into the middle of Gibraltar. The lack of surveillance in Spain and hints of some Mediterranean sloppiness at the border itself were the favourite explanations (Charles Huart was the detective constable posted to the border that day to check the passport of everyone who entered, but somehow Savage managed to drive through).

But was it a mistake, an accident? One witness thought not. According to Detective Chief Inspector Joseph Ullger, the head of Gibraltar's Special Branch, the authorities 'were concerned to gather evidence . . . Members of the [British] security service had said that they don't normally give evidence in court . . . so the [police] commissioner spelled it out that evidence was absolutely vital for the subsequent trial of the terrorists.'

McGrory: You said the only way for the operation to succeed was to allow the terrorists to come in?

Ullger: We had the police officers who were going to identify these people, SAS people . . . to assist us in the arrest, so I did not see problems at all. It would have been a problem if we'd told the police officers on duty at the frontier because unfortunately word would have got around . . . and I think there was an absolute need for extreme confidentiality.

McGrory: But you told the Spanish officers?

Ullger: Yes . . . the Spaniards were told because we required the technical advantages, facilities, which they had with computers, simply because of that.

McGrory: But you didn't tell the officers on the Gibraltar side, even to look for a passport in the name of Coyne?

Ullger: No sir, we did not.

Only two conclusions are possible from Ullger's testimony: either the Gibraltar authorities did not seriously believe Savage's car contained a bomb, or that they did, and for several hours risked the lives of Gibraltar's population so that they might gather evidence and make three arrests (remembering Lord Justice Gibson's definition of the word), which legal precedent had established as lawful, and which domestic or international opinion would hardly have found controversial given the presence of a large bomb parked near a school and a Jewish old people's home. Could there really have been a bomb activated by button? The question, finally, was immaterial.

11

But what if Savage's car contained a bomb?

Apparently undetected at the border, Savage then parked his car some time between noon and 1 p.m. Some understanding of the operation awaiting him is suggested by the number of people who spotted him *once* he had entered the town centre.

Watcher N was one of a number of people from MI5 who were meant to study the target area, the car-park outside Ince's Hall, where the bomb was expected. Watcher N said that he had a 'good view of the area, a very good view.' At 12.45 a white Renault 5 pulled into the car-park; the driver was a young man, who remained in the car for two or three minutes. A man was later seen to be wandering near the car-park, and Watcher N was asked to check his identity. He discovered that the man was the driver of the Renault 5 and that it was Sean Savage. Watcher N sent his information by radio to the operations room at 2.10 p.m., and then followed Savage 'for a considerable period.' Savage walked up and down the lanes off Main Street, stopping every now and then, 'trying to draw out stares,' to see if he was being followed. At about 3 p.m., he saw McCann and Farrell who were met by Savage. They were about 150 yards from the car.

Albert Viagas, a Gibraltar constable, was also watching the target area from the offices of Hambros Bank at one end of the car-park. Several other watchers had gathered in the same building. Viagas had two cameras and a radio—his job was to record all movements within the target zone. He did not see Savage drive in, but remembered hearing that at 12.30 p.m. a radio message had said that he had parked. A member of the security forces had commented that 'the driver had taken time and fiddled with something between the seats.' Viagas noted that the man reappeared between 2.00 and 2.30 p.m., walked away and then reappeared at 2.50 with the other two suspects. The three looked at the car and then disappeared again. Headquarters wanted the identities of the suspects confirmed, which the surveillance officers working beside Viagas were able to do: the three were McCann, Farrell and Savage. There were asked to provide further confirmation by a closer inspection, which was duly done, with the suspects positively identified by 3.25 p.m., the time the three returned to their car.

Watcher H of MI5 told the court that he first saw Savage about 2 p.m., when a radio message told him that Savage was approaching his position outside the Anglican Cathedral. He saw Savage stop at the tourist office and look at the notice-board and its diary of local events. He identified him 'with no problem at all,' and then, like Watcher N, began his tour of the alley-ways dogging Savage's heels.

About the same time, Policeman P of the Gibraltar police spotted Savage and they exchanged glances in Lovers' Lane.

By 2 p.m. Savage was being watched by officers of the military, the police and British Intelligence. There were minute-by-minute reports of his progress round Gibraltar. For more than an hour several of these agents had sat studying the car that was meant to contain a bomb of terrible potential. Could they really have believed that a bomb was there in the boot? If so, would they have sat around so casually studying it? If so, would they have done so little to protect the civilian population? After the suspects were shot, it was at least thirty minutes before anyone was warned of a potential bomb, and the first instructions to clear the area were haphazard and slow. If it was reasonable to believe that the Renault contained a bomb, then surely the people who believed it behaved unreasonably. And if it was reasonable, wouldn't somebody have told the man in charge? Until nearly 3 p.m. Police Commissioner Canepa knew nothing about Savage and his car.

12

Canepa made a good impression in the witness box; silver-haired, silver-moustached, quietly spoken, he appeared a round and paternal figure. Fighting terrorism was not his game. None the less the rules of Operation Flavius put him in control, no matter that almost every aspect of the operation—its intelligence, its watchers, its troops, its technology, even the rules themselves—had arrived by aircraft from London. Officer F and Officer E swore he was in control ('I think,' Officer F said in his plummy accent, 'that the chances of me hoodwinking the commissioner are about as good as selling ice-cream to Eskimos'), and Canepa himself grew tetchy when McGrory suggested otherwise. Indeed he seemed to believe he was still in control during the twenty-five minutes when, by his own admission, he had clearly signed control over to Officer F. But that happened later in the afternoon. For most of the day Joseph Luís Canepa was nominally in control of at least a dozen SAS men, an unspecified number of British intelligence operatives, 230 Gibraltarian police and a secret operations or 'ops' room that had been set up to co-ordinate the entire venture.

In control, but rather badly informed. Part of the trouble lay in the sophisticated radio system the military had imported for the operation. The system had two networks—tactical for the SAS soldiers, surveillance for the MI5 watchers—both of which were controlled from the ops room. It was clever, versatile equipment. The watchers and soldiers on the streets could switch into each other's networks; they had tiny microphones stuck to their collars and even smaller ear-pieces stuck in their ears; to transmit they simply pushed a button on their wrist-watches and mumbled into their shirts.

It was unfortunate that Commissioner Canepa could not hear a word. Officer E and Officer F swore that he could if he had wanted to—the information was audible in the ops room. But Canepa, who gave his evidence first, said that all the tactical and surveillance business was conducted by operators with ear-phones, who sat at different desks.

In any case, at 12.30 p.m. Canepa left the ops room and went home for lunch, leaving the acting deputy police commissioner, George Colombo, temporarily in command. It was of course at about that same time that Sean Savage was parking his car in the Ince's Hall car-park, but Canepa must have just missed being informed. So, too, however, did his deputy Colombo. In fact the military and surveillance officers neglected to tell Colombo about Savage for more than two hours.

At 2.30 p.m. Colombo did learn that two suspects believed to be McCann and Farrell had crossed the border. He telephoned Canepa, who stayed at lunch. Then at 2.50 p.m. Colombo was at last informed Savage was in town as well and that he had met McCann and Farrell; all three had been seen looking at the car: 'It was highly suspected that it was a car bomb.' He telephoned Canepa again, and this time the commissioner dismissed prospects of a prolonged siesta and made his way back to the operations room.

What happened in the operations room during the next forty minutes is far from clear, but it would seem that there were some differences of opinion between the police, Canepa and Colombo, and the military, SAS Officer E and Officer F. Under the rules of Operation Flavius the SAS soldiers on the ground had to receive control from the police before they could make their arrests. This required Canepa or his appointed deputy to sign a document which read:

> I have considered the terrorist situation in Gibraltar and have been fully briefed on the military plan with firearms. I request that you proceed with the military option which may include the use of lethal force for the preservation of life.

Canepa or his deputy would be expected to give this to Officer F, who would give the go-ahead to Officer E, the tactical commander of the troops on the ground. After the arrests had been made, Officer F would return control to the police by signing a second form:

> A military assault force completed the military option in respect of the terrorist ASU [active service unit] in Gibraltar and returns control to the civil power.

In the event, it took some time before Canepa finally signed the first document and gave the SAS the control it wanted: it was not in fact until 3.40 p.m., about forty minutes after all three suspects had been seen together and positively identified by numerous watchers.

During the inquest Canepa always insisted that there was no pre-arranged or pre-determined point of arrest, but questions were bound to arise—and perhaps were anticipated—about the forty-minute delay. According to Canepa an arrest had 'nearly been made' before he got to the ops room at 3.00 p.m., when Colombo was still in charge. Soldier A and Soldier B, however, said in court that control had been passed to them twice before 3.40 p.m., and was twice withdrawn.

Why was it withdrawn? Canepa and Colombo said that on the first occasion (they denied a second or third) that, from the direction the suspects were walking, the people in the operations room thought they were not leaving the car after all, that they were going back. At the time, Officer E, along with Soldier A and Soldier B, said the same thing: permission for an arrest had been granted and then rescinded. Real doubt at this moment seems to have existed about a bomb in the Renault.

Soldier C and Soldier D told a different story. Between 2.50 and 3.00, they were in Trafalgar Cemetery, about a minute's walk from the car-park, when the three suspects strolled past. Officer E told Soldiers C and D to get out of the area and make for the airport. It is not clear why; ten or fifteen minutes later, they heard on the radio that Soldiers A and B had been given control for the first time and had been asked to 'apprehend the terrorists,' who were, by then, returning to their car. Soldiers C and D were told to turn back. And, as they did so, control was then withdrawn.

Why this reluctance to allow the military to make its arrests? The evidence suggests that it had nothing to do with the direction in which the three suspects may or may not have been walking. It was because Canepa had returned to the ops room. According to Colombo, one of his chief's priorities was to order that the suspects be 'formally identified.' No watcher or soldier was in any doubt about their identities by then—even Colombo thought they were 'eighty per cent certain'—but none the less two watchers left the hide-out in the Hambros Bank and confirmed the identities of the three around 3.25 p.m.

Soon after, the three began to walk north down Main Street, suggesting to Officers E and F that they were leaving the car behind and making for the border (an oddly certain conclusion: they could simply have been making for the centre of town for a drink). According to Officer E and his soldiers in the field, control again passed to them and was again rescinded, this time more swiftly than before, because, in the words of Officer E, 'The police commissioner wanted to be one hundred per cent sure of the identities of the three terrorists before any arrest was made.' Canepa seems to have been a troubled man; by the account of other witnesses he had been requesting and receiving confirmations of identity for about twenty minutes by now. And yet Colombo's 'eighty per cent' would have been more than good enough for most policemen in most circumstances, and his military and intelligence advisors, who knew much more about Irish terrorists than he did, seemed absolutely sure. What could have been troubling the commissioner? Wrongful arrest? Surely not; three badly scared tourists would have been the only result. Unless, of course, they were to be arrested in Lord Justice Gibson's sense of the word.

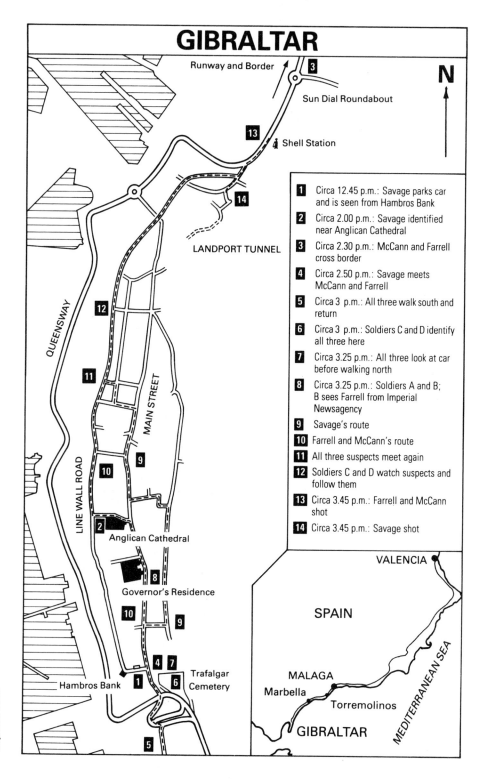

GIBRALTAR

Runway and Border

3

Sun Dial Roundabout

N

13

🚏 Shell Station

14

LANDPORT TUNNEL

1 Circa 12.45 p.m.: Savage parks car and is seen from Hambros Bank

2 Circa 2.00 p.m.: Savage identified near Anglican Cathedral

3 Circa 2.30 p.m.: McCann and Farrell cross border

4 Circa 2.50 p.m.: Savage meets McCann and Farrell

5 Circa 3 p.m.: All three walk south and return

6 Circa 3 p.m.: Soldiers C and D identify all three here

7 Circa 3.25 p.m.: All three look at car before walking north

8 Circa 3.25 p.m.: Soldiers A and B; B sees Farrell from Imperial Newsagency

9 Savage's route

10 Farrell and McCann's route

11 All three suspects meet again

12 Soldiers C and D watch suspects and follow them

13 Circa 3.45 p.m.: Farrell and McCann shot

14 Circa 3.45 p.m.: Savage shot

QUEENSWAY

12

11

MAIN STREET

LINE WALL ROAD

9

10

2

Anglican Cathedral

8

Governor's Residence

10

9

4 **7**

1

6

Hambros Bank

Trafalgar Cemetery

5

VALENCIA ●

SPAIN

MALAGA
Marbella ●
Torremolinos

GIBRALTAR

MEDITERRANEAN SEA

13

Events began to move quickly.

Soldier C and Soldier D, having almost got to the airport, now returned towards the centre and were sheltering behind the Mobil petrol station in Line Wall Road. The three suspects passed walking towards the border. Farrell kept looking over her shoulder. Soldier C and Soldier D began to follow. For the next few minutes soldiers and suspects were in sight of each other. Soldier C and Soldier D were wearing loose shirts, casually covering the nine-millimetre Browning pistols stuck in their trouser waistbands.

At 3.40 p.m. Canepa signed his paper and gave it to Officer F who handed it to Officer E, who then devolved control to his men in the field. According to their evidence, the time and place of arrest were now entirely in their hands. Soldier A and Soldier B took a short-cut through the Landport Tunnel; Soldier C and Soldier D continued walking along the road; both ways were about to meet at the complicated junction where the town of Gibraltar draws together its few roads and sends them forward towards Spain in a short stretch of grandiose dual carriageway: Winston Churchill Avenue. Soldiers and watchers told the court that the three suspects stopped at this junction on Winston Churchill Avenue; some evidence said that Savage and McCann exchanged newspapers here. Two pairs of SAS troops now approached them from behind, all four utterly convinced, so they told the court, that any hesitation on their part could mean carnage a mile to the south.

Approaching Danny McCann, Soldier A was convinced that if he could kill him, he would prevent the slaughter of innocents. His vision was intense:

> At that stage there I thought the man McCann was definitely going to go for a button. Uppermost in my mind . . . was the bomb and the de-bussing area. On that particular Sunday itself I noticed a couple of ships in the harbour, quite a few people around about the area of Main Street. Uppermost in my mind was this bomb. If he had gone for the button to press the button which would

have detonated the bomb which was in the car or that was believed to be in the car . . . So . . . as I said, I was drawing my weapon. I fired at McCann one round into his back.

Soldier A's conviction about the existence of the bomb was deeply inculcated. But it was not nearly as strong as the conviction felt by Soldier C—which emerged when McGrory began asking him about Farrell. How long had he had her under observation?

Soldier C: On and off for an hour.

McGrory: And during which time Miss Farrell was showing this . . . alertness or nervousness about surveillance?

Soldier C: Very much so.

McGrory: However, you and your surveillance teams were so good at your jobs that she doesn't appear to have twigged, so to speak, that she was being watched closely?

Soldier C: No sir. Well they had just laid a bomb . . .

McGrory: Had just what?

Soldier C: Had just laid a bomb in the Ince's Hall area.

McGrory: No, they had not.

Soldier C [angrily]: I was told by [Officer] E!

McGrory: You are just after saying they had just laid a bomb. You know perfectly well they had not laid a bomb.

Soldier C: I was briefed on that day and categorically told there was a definite bomb in Ince's Hall. I can only operate from that information at that moment in time.

McGrory: It turned out to be rubbish, of course?

Soldier C: At that moment in time I can only react to that information.

McGrory: And at all times you were acting with the information that had been fed into you by [Officer] E?

Soldier C: Fed into me by [Officer] E, yes.

McGrory: Can we get it clear that you are not saying now that there was a bomb?

Soldier C: I don't understand what you are saying.

McGrory: It can't be the fault of my [Ulster] accent this time. I am saying to you, you are not telling his Honour and the jury now that you still believe there was a bomb?

Soldier C: I am not talking about that. I am talking about information I had; on the day there was a bomb in Ince's Hall.

McGrory: I am talking [about] now . . . and would you tell me whether you now believe that now as you stand there, that there was a bomb?

Soldier C: I still believe that there is a bomb in Gibraltar.

The Coroner [trying to clarify]: He still *believed.*

Some conversation between McGrory and Laws, the government's counsel, occurred at this point. Then the coroner intervened again: 'Put it directly to him. "Do you know that there was no bomb?"'

Soldier C: [at last] At this point in time I'd be a fool not to know.

Where did this strange certainty come from?

14

The night before the killings, at the secret midnight advisory meeting, there was a discussion about the two kinds of detonation— timer and radio-controlled. The police witnesses who attended that meeting—Commissioner Canepa, Detective Chief Inspector Ullger, Policeman Q and Policeman R—recalled that a timer *had not* been ruled out. But members of the SAS—both the officers and Soldiers A, B, C and D—attending the same meeting, all believed, and not just believed but *knew*, 'one hundred per cent', that the bomb would be radio-controlled, a 'button job'. Further, they believed that all three suspects would be carrying transmitters or 'buttons'.

One of the small revelations of the inquest was that on certain kinds of operations, including this one, SAS units take an army lawyer with them. The lawyer attending their legal needs in Gibraltar had, it transpired, drawn up the document which Canepa signed to give control to the military. He also accompanied the four soldiers when they went to hand over their guns and their spare ammunition at the Gibraltar police station after the shooting. And he also secured permission, from the colony's deputy attorney-general, that the unit could leave that night for the United Kingdom without first making any statements to the local police. In fact it was not until 15 March, after several sessions with the army lawyer, that the soldiers made statements to British policemen who were acting on behalf of their colleagues in Gibraltar. And it was months before it was even decided that the soldiers would 'volunteer' to attend their trial. No doubt the SAS lawyers had the opportunity to clarify any confusion in the soldiers' minds during this period; which is their right.

Was it reasonable that the soldiers hold these beliefs about the 'button' so firmly? Yes; they had been instilled by their commanding officers. Were the mistaken beliefs reasonable in themselves? Only Mr O knows, but he offered scant evidence to support them. Did they grow more reasonable as the afternoon of 6 March wore on? Hardly, though the crown tried hard to show so.

The important evidence: First, Savage had been seen 'fiddling with something in the car' after he parked it. The watcher alleged to have seen this fiddling (perhaps a seat-belt?) never turned up at the inquest. Second, the three suspects 'stared hard' or 'looked intently' at the car. Hardly proof of evil intention, far less a radio-controlled bomb. Third, the Renault had 'an old aerial' and yet was 'a relatively new car.' Several official witnesses latched on to this conjunction, which came originally from Officer G, the bomb-disposal expert. At about 3.25 G was sent from the ops room to inspect the car, about which he found nothing untoward apart from the aerial. But when the aerial was produced in court it turned out to be a remarkably unsuspicious piece of wire.

15

6 March 1988. Soldier A and Soldier B emerged from the Landport Tunnel with a female witness, known as Watcher J. Soon they saw McCann, Farrell and Savage standing together just north of the zebra crossing on Corral Road. They were talking and smiling. According to Soldier A, Savage broke away from the group and started to walk up towards the soldiers, actually bumping into Soldier A's shoulder as he moved past. Watcher J turned and followed Savage.

Soldier A and Soldier B pressed on towards Farrell and McCann, who were now walking towards the border. According to their evidence, Soldier A followed McCann on the inside of the pavement, while Soldier B took the outer position behind Farrell. The soldiers started to walk fast—'a controlled brisk pace'. By the time Farrell and McCann had walked a hundred yards and were in front of the Shell petrol station, Soldiers A and B were only a few feet behind them. Then McCann looked back—the glance that, by this evidence, killed him, killed all of them, and started a small procession of Belfast coffins.

Soldier A: He had a smile on his face and he looked over at me. We literally had what I would call eye-to-eye contact. We looked directly at each other, and the smile went off McCann's face, and, it's hard to describe, it's almost like McCann had a realization of actually who I was, or I was a threat to him. The look on his face was of alertness and he was very aware. So this came over his face and at that stage then I was just going to shout a warning to stop . . . and at the same time I was drawing my pistol. I went to shout 'Stop!' whether it [the word] actually came out I honestly don't know. I went to shout 'Stop!' and the events overtook the warning. The look on McCann's face, the alertness . . . then all of a sudden his right arm, right elbow, actually moved aggressively across the front of his body . . .

The button.

Soldier A then shot McCann once in the back. 'I then, out of the corner of my eye . . . [saw that] Farrell had a bag under her left armpit at this stage. She had actually moved to the right and was grabbing her bag.'

Another button.

Soldier A then shot Farrell once in the back before switching his fire back to McCann, who was now falling to the ground. He aimed once at his body and twice at his head.

Soldier A did not hear Soldier B fire, though Soldier B heard Soldier A's shots. Soldier B said that as Soldier A was the senior partner he expected him to initiate the arrest. He heard 'a startled yell' to his right and in a split second 'firing, bargh, bargh, firing'. Soldier B was drawing his own weapon at the time. 'At the same instant again Farrell, who I was still watching intently, made a sharp move to her right, and she was carrying a shoulder bag which she drew across her body.'

The button.

Soldier B: I, with the information I'd been given at the time—we were told of their professionalism, their dedication, and of all the car-bombing and other information—I was intently watching Farrell . . . in my mind she made all the actions to carry out a detonation of a radio-controlled device. Uppermost in my mind at that time, sir [to the coroner], was the lives of the general public in that area.'

Soldier B thought he fired one or two rounds at Farrell before he switched his fire to McCann—'Because I didn't know whether Soldier A had been shot, and I perceived McCann as being an equal threat to myself, Gibraltarians and my comrades.' When he returned his aim to Farrell she was going down, but he continued to fire because, he said, he still couldn't see her hands. He did not know how many rounds he had fired at each person, but he fired seven in all and did not miss, he said, with any of them. 'I carried on firing until both the terrorists were laying on the floor, their arms were away from any device or bag, and I decided that they were no longer a threat.'

The twelve shots fired at the Shell station had, according to Soldier C and Soldier D, an instant effect on Savage. He was about 150 yards away and walking back towards town, going up the same path to the tunnel which Soldier A and Soldier B had recently come down. Soldier C and Soldier D had caught up with him and were, according to Soldier C, about five or six feet behind him. Soldier D was to the left and slightly ahead.

Soldier C: There were a lot of people coming towards us . . . My intention at this stage was to effect the arrest but as I was moving forward there were shots to my left rear [at Shell] . . . and when this happened Savage spun round very fast. As he spun round I shouted, 'Stop!' At the time I was shouting, he went down with his right arm to the area of his jacket pocket.

Another button.

Soldier C: At this stage I fired, because at this moment in time it had been confirmed from [Officer] E that there was a device, a bomb, at the Ince's Hall area which could be detonated by one of these three terrorists, more likely to be Savage, because earlier he had been seen in that vehicle, playing around in the front, leaving the vehicle.

Soldier C fired six rounds at 'the mass' of Savage's body and thought that four hit him in the chest and two in the head, as Savage went 'spiralling down . . . like a corkscrew' through his arc of fire. He stopped firing 'as soon as Savage had hit the ground, his arms had flung back to the side and I was sure, at that moment in time, that he was no longer a threat to initiate that device.'

Soldier D said he pushed a woman away with his left hand and drew his Browning with his right, to get 'a clear line of arrest' as his counsel Hucker called it. He had not drawn his gun when Savage spun round and Soldier C shouted stop.

Soldier D: At this stage I had to make a decision as to what my actions would be, and uppermost in my mind at the time was what had been confirmed to me by [Officer] E. He told me there was a bomb . . . I believed that Savage had a detonator and he was going to detonate the device. With all the innocent people up in the area I had to make a decision. There was gun-fire to my left and to the rear. Again, I didn't know what that was. I didn't know if Soldiers A and B had been shot by McCann and Farrell, and I also had a threat to the people who were around me at the time . . . At this stage I had to make a decision, and it was in milliseconds I drew my pistol and I fired at Savage.

And went on firing at him; nine shots as he twisted and fell, all aimed at the centre of his body, apart from the last two which were aimed at his head—'just before he became still, just as he reached the ground.' Soldier C estimated that their total of fifteen shots had been fired from within three to five seconds—fast work with non-automatic pistols—but could not be sure if Soldier D went on firing after he had stopped.

None of this, of course, was supposed to happen. The court heard how the SAS had practised their arrest procedure. Pistols would be drawn, a challenge shouted and the suspects made to lie on the ground with their hands away from their bodies until Gibraltar policemen arrived with handcuffs. Four or five times the challenge itself burst from behind the curtain over the witness box. STOP . . . POLICE . . . HANDS UP. Few in the court (including the coroner, as he later confessed) had understood this challenge when Officer E first demonstrated it. Consonants disappeared, vowels were mangled—it was no more than the kind of frightening noise which professional soldiers perfect on the barrack-square. In any case the challenge was something of a luxury. As Soldier D said, 'In our rules of engagement, if we thought the threat was so great . . . we had no need to give a warning. We knew the fact the bomb was there. We knew he [Savage] could well be carrying the device to detonate the bomb. With him making such violent movements . . . in fact we didn't even need to give him a warning.'

McGrory: Why did you give him it then?

Soldier D: Because we gave him the benefit of the doubt. We told him to stop. He didn't stop. He carried on with the movement.

Loud noises frighten people. They tend to move. No soldier could explain to the inquest, however, why the dead had moved as they were alleged to have done. No buttons, no guns, but three distinct movements, all of them lethal. Was there anything Savage, Farrell and McCann could have done to prevent themselves from being killed that day, apart from rewriting the history of their last few months alive? One thing had always been clear. There was never an intention to shoot to immobilize: soldiers are trained to fire and go on firing until they kill, and in this case they needed to expunge life, to stop the possibility of 'contrived movement', in Hucker's phrase, as quickly as possible. But McGrory wondered what would have happened if Savage, in the middle of the firing, had shouted, 'Stop!

I surrender!' Would Soldier D have carried on killing him?

Soldier D: I would have carried on firing until I believed he was no longer a threat.

McGrory: Even if words of surrender like that had been uttered like that?

Soldier D: He may well have said that and pressed the button at the same time.

McGrory: The startled man was wheeling, and the shout and the shot had come on top of each other. What chance had he to surrender?

Soldier D: He had been given the chance. He had been told to stop and he didn't.

McGrory: You didn't even finish the warning.

Soldier D: Because we didn't have the time to finish the warning.

McGrory: I am suggesting to you, soldier, that you appointed yourself Lord High Executioner of Mr Savage on this day.

Soldier D: That is definitely not true.

16

By Officer E's reckoning Savage, Farrell and McCann had died at 3.47 p.m. He was in the ops room with Canepa, Officer F and others when his men radioed in—somewhere between 3.47 and 3.48 p.m.—that the 'apprehension of the terrorists had taken place.' Officer E said he wasn't sure what this implied—though clarification would surely have been easy enough—and so he left and went to the scene with Detective Chief Inspector Ullger of the Special Branch. By 4 p.m. he had confirmed that the three were dead and that the SAS soldiers were 'safely out of the area'. Canepa himself did not hear about the killings until 4.05 p.m., his first definite information since he handed over control twenty-five minutes before. One minute later Officer F signed the document which restored control to the civil power.

17

There is in police methodology a universal principle known as the preservation of the scene of the crime. It was applied sparingly on 6 March. Within minutes, the Gibraltar police had corrupted, if not quite destroyed, any chance that the killings could be properly reconstructed by the higher standards of legal proof. The spent cartridges were collected without first marking where they had been found. The bodies were removed without first photographing them *in situ*. No one bothered to chalk around the outlines of Farrell and McCann; without the pictures of Douglas Celecia, an amateur photographer whose home overlooks the scene, the inquest may never have known precisely how or where they had fallen (Celecia's photographs, which appear in these pages, were later seized by the police and restored to him, only after a legal action, with every face whited out).

The bodies were then removed to the morgue of the Royal Naval Hospital. A senior pathologist, Professor Alan Watson of Glasgow University, arrived around lunch-time the next day to perform the autopsy. It wasn't an easy job. The hospital had a mobile X-ray machine, but he was never given access to it; X-rays could have traced the track of bullets through the bodies. The clothing had already been removed; torn fabric can help determine entry and exit wounds, while the spread of blood stains could indicate whether the three were upright or prone when they were shot. He found the photographs taken in the morgue inadequate— the police photographer had not been under his direction—and there was no surgical help. Subsequently he was not given any copies of the ballistic and forensic reports, nor the reports on the blood samples he had submitted in London on his return.

McGrory expressed puzzlement.

'Yes,' said Professor Watson, 'it is a puzzle to me too. I am just giving you the facts.'

But wasn't there normally close co-operation between the pathologist and the forensic scientist?

'Yes,' said Watson, 'but here, I repeat, I have had none.'

Why not?

'I cannot answer that question.'

71

'Are you saying,' McGrory asked, 'that at no stage in the last six months did you become aware that, for instance, it was a matter of importance in this case that it is alleged that some, if not all, of these people were shot as they lay on the ground?'

'Yes, [but] I had expected that you would put those questions to the . . . forensic scientist.'

The forensic scientist was David Pryor of the London Metropolitan Police. He appeared in court on 27 September. Professor Watson had appeared on 8 September. The gap between their appearances made it impossible to combine their complementary evidence, blurring thereby a vital—maybe the most vital—question in the case: Did the wounds, the clothing and the bullets bear out the stories of the soldiers?

Like Watson, however, Pryor had been handicapped. The blood-soaked clothes had been dispatched to him in bags. 'The clothing was in such a condition when I received it,' said Pryor, 'that accurate determination of which was an entry site and which an exit site was very difficult.' What Pryor could say, from powder marks found on Farrell's jacket and Savage's shirt, was that a gun had been fired about three feet from Farrell's back and about four feet to six feet from Savage's chest. And of two bullets found in Savage's head, one came from the gun of Soldier C and the other from that of Soldier D. Watson's evidence, however, proved in the end to be more important than Pryor's, and taken together with 'strike marks'—impressions left by bullets—in the ground it casts a good deal of doubt on the soldiers' stories.

The first body Watson examined was Mairead Farrell's. Farrell had three entry wounds in the back and three exit wounds in the chest. The back wounds were all within about two-and-a-half inches of each other—a cluster—and neater and smaller than the chest wounds, which were higher in the body. The five wounds to her face and neck were produced by two bullet tracks: one from the left cheek to the hair-line below the left ear, producing an intermediate hole just below the left ear; one on the right neck beneath the chin to the left neck just above the collar line. The head wounds were superficial. Farrell had been killed by gunshot wounds to the heart and liver. Watson thought that Farrell must either have had 'the entire body, or at least the upper part of the body, turned towards the shooter' when she was shot in the face and had then been shot in the back as she was going down. Farrell's height was only five feet one inch, said McGrory, so the upward trajectory of the bullets in her back would mean that the gunman would have to be kneeling, or Farrell would need to be close to the ground. Watson agreed.

'Or on her face?'

'Yes.'

McCann had two entry wounds to the back, again close together, and two exits in the chest. Again the trajectory was upward. He had a hole without an exit in the lower left jaw and extensive damage to the back left side of the brain caused by a bullet which appeared to have entered at the top left back of his head and exited in his left neck above the hair-line. The hole in the jaw could have been a ricochet or a bullet which had first passed through Farrell. The bullets in the back and the back of the head would all have been lethal. Watson suggested that the wound in the jaw stunned him and the rest were fired at his back and head 'when he was down or very far down.'

Savage was a mess. His twenty-nine wounds, said Watson, suggested 'a frenzied attack'. He had seven wounds to the head, five to the back, one to each shoulder, five to the chest, three to the abdomen ('and lying there in the depth of the navel itself was a piece of grey distorted metal presumed to be a bullet'), two to the left thigh, two to the right arm, one superficial to the left arm and two to the left hand. Watson recorded the cause of death as fractures of the skull and cerebral lacerations, with a contribution from gunshot wounds to the lungs. He thought sixteen or eighteen bullets had struck Savage, which is at least one more than Soldiers C and Soldier D said they fired. He said that of the seven head wounds, five were probably entries. 'But bullets, with respect, are extremely difficult . . . a bullet does not simply do what you imagine.' The exits and entries to the chest and back were difficult to establish with certainty.

At first sight, Watson's evidence seems to support two civilian witnesses—Mrs Carmen Proetta and Mrs Josie Celecia—in their earlier statements to the press and television that Farrell and McCann were shot from close range as they lay on the ground. That could account for the clusters in the back, the powder marks on Farrell's jacket and the upward trajectory of bullets fired by a gunman standing nearer to their feet. What this supposition overlooks, however, is that all the evidence, including Celecia's pictures, suggest that Farrell and McCann fell backwards, face up.

The wounds to Farrell's face and neck, on the other hand, do support evidence in court from several civilian witnesses that one or more of the gunmen fired from the road rather than the pavement, where Soldiers A and B claimed they stood. She seems to have turned back and to the left—a bullet tearing through the left side of her face from cheek to neck—from her position at the edge of the pavement. In which case the bag on her left shoulder, which contained the notional detonating device, could hardly have been hidden from the gunman's view.

In Savage's case the contradictions are quite impossible to reconcile. Soldier C thought he hit him twice in the head, accidentally, as he fell through the soldier's arc of fire. Soldier D said he fired twice at his head as Savage was close to the ground. Sure enough, a bullet from each gun was found in his skull, and the other two bullets could have gone clean through. But the Gibraltar police, in an unusual moment of efficiency, had circled four strike marks within the chalk outline of Savage's head. Watson saw a photograph of these strike marks for the first time when McGrory showed it to him in court. Did it look as though those bullets were fired into his head as he lay there?

'Yes, that would be reasonable.'

18

This is not the only problem with the death of Savage. Savage died in a busy area—6 March was Gibraltar's first fine Sunday of the spring, with families strolling in and out of town through the Landport Tunnel. Soldiers C and D themselves estimated there were about thirty people in the vicinity. Yet the coroner's office could find only three civilian witnesses to Savage's death, two of whom had been found originally by Thames Television. The picture of the shooting that emerges from them, and from the four MI5 watchers who were also close by, has some extraordinary gaps (see Diagram One).

DIAGRAM ONE: SAVAGE

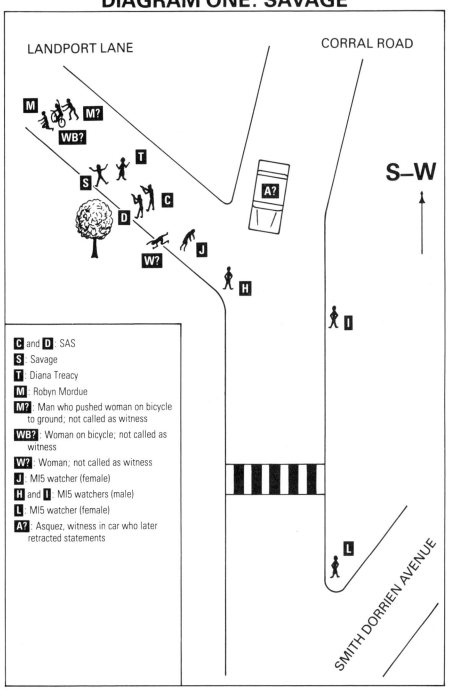

LANDPORT LANE

CORRAL ROAD

S–W

C and **D**: SAS
S: Savage
T: Diana Treacy
M: Robyn Mordue
M?: Man who pushed woman on bicycle to ground; not called as witness
WB?: Woman on bicycle; not called as witness
W?: Woman; not called as witness
J: MI5 watcher (female)
H and **I**: MI5 watchers (male)
L: MI5 watcher (female)
A?: Asquez, witness in car who later retracted statements

SMITH DORRIEN AVENUE

Diagram: Peter Covill

Kenneth Asquez, a twenty-year-old bank clerk, alleged last April that he saw a man with his foot on Savage's chest, firing into him at point-blank range two or three times. Asquez made the claim in two statements, one hand-written and another made before a lawyer, which he refused to sign because, he said, he wanted to protect his identity. Thames Television used seventy-two words from his statements. But at the inquest Asquez—a surprise witness, given his previous anonymity—said he had invented his account under 'pressure' and 'offers of money', the first unspecified and the second unquantified (he received none, in any case). Sir Joshua Hassan, the colony's most distinguished lawyer and former chief minister, represented him in court. Asquez said he was 'confused' about which parts of his statements were true and which parts he'd made up. The coroner said that, retracted or not, his first account should still be considered by the jury.

Then there is Robyn Arthur Mordue. He was a British holiday-maker, walking towards Savage in Landport Lane when the shooting started and he was pushed to the ground by a woman on a bicycle (herself pushed by a third party). He saw Savage fall at the same time. The shots stopped for a time, and then resumed as Mordue struggled to his feet; as he ran for cover behind a car, he looked back to see a man standing over Savage and pointing down with a gun. Mordue was a confused (and perhaps frightened) witness; coroner and counsel examined him ten times before he was released from his oath. He may also have been a confused and frightened witness before he arrived in Gibraltar: in the weeks before the inquest, he received a number of threatening phone calls ('Bastard . . . stay away'). His telephone number is ex-directory.

Diana Treacy, another Gibraltar bank employee, told the court she saw two men running towards her, the second with a gun. After she was passed by the first man, who turned out to be Savage, the gunman opened fire, about six feet in front of her. While Savage was on the ground, she saw the gunman fire another three, four or five shots into him. Professional observers close by managed to see even less.

Watcher J, the woman surveillance officer from MI5, followed Savage round the corner and turned away when he spun round, to avoid eye-contact. She neither saw the shooting, nor heard any of the fifteen to eighteen shots fired. Yet she was only fifteen feet away.

'Is that not,' McGrory asked her during the inquest, 'a very remarkable thing?'

'It may be, sir, but I did not hear them.'

Watcher H, the surveillance officer who accompanied Soldiers C and D, saw Savage spin round with 'an expression of amazement, a quite intense expression'. Then Watcher H too turned away and ran back down the road to warn people to take cover. He saw none of the shooting. When he looked back he saw that Savage was on the ground and that Soldier C and Soldier D had 'stood back' to the right of the lane.

Watcher I said he heard gun-fire in the lane and walked a few paces to have a look. He saw 'one or two shots being fired, by which time the terrorist Savage was on the ground.' He left the scene immediately.

Watcher L, another woman from MI5, heard gun-fire from the lane and 'got to the ground, a natural reaction.'

The woman on the bicycle and the man (possibly a watcher) who pushed her were never identified. Neither was the woman whom Soldier D pushed with his left hand. The only complete account of Savage's death comes from the people who say they killed him.

19

Commissioner Canepa contended that there was no predetermined point of arrest: that everyone happened to arrive on the scene just before the shooting started. Diagram Two illustrates just how many people happened to turn up—at least of those we know. Policeman P, Policeman Q and Policeman R are all members of the Gibraltar police force, armed with .38 Smith and Wesson revolvers. They just happened to form a circle around the scene of the shooting. Policeman P hitched a lift from a foreign-registered Mercedes, and Policemen Q and R rode by their motorbikes. There were others. Watcher K of MI5 had been hiding behind the hedge for some time. There was also Detective Constable Charles Huart, who, after his fruitless day's work examining passports at the border, having failed to identify Savage (and later Farrell and McCann), happened more or less by accident to show up. There was also a police car that parked opposite the petrol station, from which four men came, crossing the barrier which divides the two carriageways; they are Inspector Joseph Revagliatte, Sergeant Emilio Acris, PC Ian Howes and the police car's driver, PC Clive Borrell.

All four policemen told the inquest that, like the vast majority of Gibraltar's police, they knew nothing of Operation Flavius. Their presence at the shootings was fortuitous, they said. And yet the inquest also heard the theory that they had caused, or at least prompted, the shootings to begin. Theirs is the story of the accidental siren that Carmen Proetta and Stephen Bullock heard.

According to Inspector Revagliatte, he and his men were making a routine patrol of the colony when at 3.41 p.m. they got a call to return urgently to the central police station. The car was stuck in traffic, and, as the call was urgent, the driver switched on the siren. Just past the Shell station, Revagliatte heard 'what appeared to be shots,' turned and saw two bodies on the pavement. He radioed the police station, and the operator logged the call there at 3.42 p.m.: 'Control, we have firing incident at Shell petrol station.'

The police car went swiftly round the roundabout and then headed back towards the Shell station. During this short journey— thirty seconds at most—Revagliatte told his men to divert traffic from the scene of the shooting. Before they were dispersed, however, all four went over or around the central barrier and towards the bodies. Given that all four were unarmed and had just seen two people gunned down by unknown assailants, their behaviour was certainly both prompt and gallant.

For Mr Hucker, counsel for the soldiers, Revagliatte's testimony was a splendid instrument, accommodating some of the most stubborn and awkward evidence of the inquest. First, why is there only one uniformed policeman in Douglas Celecia's photographs? Because the others have gone off to do their traffic duties. Second, why did McCann suddenly glance backwards in the suspicious or frightened way that resulted in him being shot? Because he and Farrell were panicked by the siren. And finally and most importantly, why did Carmen Proetta believe that she saw

DIAGRAM TWO: McCANN AND FARRELL

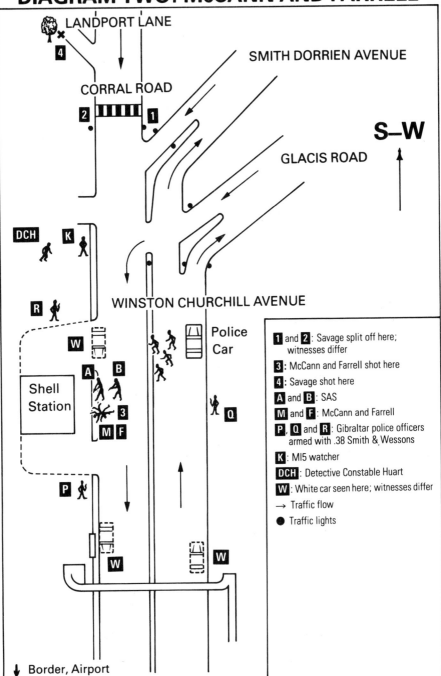

LANDPORT LANE

4

SMITH DORRIEN AVENUE

CORRAL ROAD

2 **1**

S–W

GLACIS ROAD

DCH **K**

R

WINSTON CHURCHILL AVENUE

W

Police Car

A **B**

Shell Station

3

M **F**

Q

P

W

W

1 and **2**: Savage split off here; witnesses differ

3: McCann and Farrell shot here

4: Savage shot here

A and **B**: SAS

M and **F**: McCann and Farrell

P, **Q** and **R**: Gibraltar police officers armed with .38 Smith & Wessons

K: MI5 watcher

DCH: Detective Constable Huart

W: White car seen here; witnesses differ

→ Traffic flow

● Traffic lights

↓ Border, Airport

Diagram: Peter Covill

armed men attack McCann and Farrell from over the barrier? Because what she saw, and got muddled by, was a group of uniformed, unarmed policemen jump over the barrier some seconds after Soldiers A and B shot Farrell and McCann from the footpath.

Again and again, the counsel for the SAS allowed Revagliatte to demonstrate how his involvement in the killings was accidental:

Hucker: Inspector, I am going to ask you some questions on behalf of Soldiers A to G. The first matter is what your knowledge was of the operation to arrest the terrorists on 6 March. When you came on shift at three o'clock or thereabouts, did you know anything about that operation at all?

Revagliatte: Nothing at all.

Hucker: You thought that life in Gibraltar was totally normal, that what was happening between you and the border was the same as happened any other day of the week?

Revagliatte: Exactly.

In November, eight weeks after Inspector Revagliatte gave this evidence, a startling fact emerged. His name appears on the secret operational order prepared by police Commissioner Canepa for Operation Flavius that was read by certain unnamed police officers at the midnight briefing between 5 and 6 March. The order assigns him a vital role—officer in charge of the two police firearms teams. Each team consisted of three armed policemen, and one consisted of the witnesses known as Policemen P, Q and R, the same policemen who happened to form a circle round the scene of the shooting. Had this fact been disclosed to the court, the jury would would have been asked to conclude:

1. That while Policemen P, Q and R had attended the midnight briefing, their commanding officer for the operation, Revagliatte, had not.

2. That while Policemen P, Q and R knew their role on 6 March, their commanding officer, Revagliatte, did not.

3. That though Revagliatte and Policemen P, Q and R appeared at the scene of the killings almost simultaneously, this was pure coincidence.

The British government may, of course, supply a simple explanation. But as I write, two weeks after the question was first raised in the Irish parliament, it has so far neglected to comment.

So what are we now to believe? If Revagliatte was knowingly involved, the official version of what happened in Winston Churchill Avenue needs to be completely re-examined. We fall back on what his testimony tended to destroy—the stubborn and awkward evidence of the civilian witnesses who first appeared on Thames Television. Carmen Proetta said at the inquest more or less what she said on television: that from her kitchen window she saw a car pull up and one uniformed policeman and three men in plain clothes get out and jump over the barrier; that at least two of the men in plain clothes appeared to have guns; that two people (McCann and Farrell), on the pavement near the Shell station, looked round and raised their hands to about head level; that one shot dropped the girl to the ground; that the man moved as if to shield or help her; that then he too went down in 'a fusillade of shots'. Behind McCann and Farrell, she also saw a fifth man with what looked like a gun; then a man with fairish hair crouched over the bodies with his hands clasped together at waist level, seemingly pointing a gun. She heard more shots. (Josie Celecia, whose husband took the photographs, made a similar observation in court: that she too saw a man standing over the bodies with his hands clasped together, his arms outstretched, pointing downwards, and that she heard bangs—bangs which the soldiers' counsel suggested came from the shooting of Savage.) Proetta then saw a second car draw up, this time on the same side of the road as the petrol station, and men in plain clothes got out and started arguing and 'gesticulating' at the fairish man, who was pulled into the second car by someone in a dark jacket and driven away.

It is worth recalling Stephen Bullock, the English lawyer strolling with his wife and child. He saw a police car stuck in traffic next to him on Smith Dorrien Avenue. He thought its siren sounded at the same time as shooting started. When he looked in the direction of the Shell station he saw a gunman firing rapidly from the edge of the road at another man, three or four feet away on the pavement, who was falling backwards with his hands raised above shoulder height. Something which looked like a heap of clothes was already on the ground.

The siren, however, may not have been a mistake. Perhaps it formed some part of the arrest plan. Shortly before the shooting started a man with a pistol stuck down his jeans pushed past Bullock, saying, 'Excuse me,' and then went on to meet a man similarly dressed and also armed, who was standing near the corner. The men looked at the shooting at the Shell station, and then ran off towards Landport Lane. They were probably Soldiers C and D. Bullock remembers that the man who pushed past looked back at the police car. 'He seemed to have some sort of interest in what the police car was doing.'

And what was that car doing?

Soldiers A and B said that they approached McCann and Farrell from behind by walking briskly along the pavement after them. They have always insisted that they were still on the pavement, side by side, when they opened fire and stayed there throughout the shooting. But if we add the accounts of these eye-witnesses to the forensic evidence—the little, that is, that survives—then at least the opening rounds came from gunmen firing from the road, not the pavement. This small difference poses large questions. Could gunmen have arrived by car? Where did Policemen P, Q and R come from? Were they not, perhaps, in the positions that they told the court? Somebody began shooting from the road not the pavement, and if, as the forensic evidence suggests, Farrell had turned to face them, then there would have been no mystery about the movements of her hand: she would have been clearly in view of the gunmen.

20

On the morning of 30 September the coroner summed up the evidence to the members of the jury and urged them to avoid the ambiguity of an open verdict. They should decide whether Savage, Farrell and McCann had been killed lawfully, 'that is justifiable, reasonable homicide,' or unlawfully, 'that is unlawful homicide.' If they were to conclude that any of the three—though only Savage was mentioned by name—had been shot on the ground simply to 'finish them off,' then that would be murder.

The jury left the court at 11.30 a.m. to consider its verdict and re-appeared again at 5.20 p.m. to say it had been unable to agree a decision. The coroner then told the members of the jury that they were 'reaching the edge' of a reasonable time to produce one, and said he would expect to see them again at 7 p.m. To some observers in the court, this sounded like a deadline. At 7.15 p.m. the jury returned again, and the foreman rose to say it had reached a verdict of lawful killing by a majority of nine to two, the smallest majority allowed.

This was hardly a vote of confidence in the behaviour of the British army on 6 March. None the less jubilation erupted in London among members and supporters of the British government. The reaction of Mr Jerry Hayes, Conservative Member of Parliament for Harlow and secretary of his party's back bench committee on Northern Ireland, was typical. 'This is wonderful news for those brave young men in the SAS who daily put their lives at risk to protect our democracy,' he told the *Daily Telegraph*. After all: 'What greater inquiry could one have than an independent inquest in an independent colony?'

21

That was two months ago now. Today in England another inquiry still continues—the inquiry into how Thames Television came to make its documentary, 'Death on the Rock'. The television company itself instigated this inquiry to appease the government; there was talk that the government might deprive the company of its broadcasting franchise. Already it has lasted twice as long as the inquest itself and its two investigators—Lord Windlesham and Mr Richard Rampton—are still taking evidence. Rampton is a barrister, a Queen's Counsel. Windlesham is a Conservative peer, a former government minister in Northern Ireland and the author of a book entitled *Broadcasting in a Free Society*: they have been charged to discover if the programme was 'responsible' and if it 'performed a public service by contributing information and insight on a controversial matter of public concern.'

W hat really happened in Gibraltar on 6 March? Many of us who gathered under the Levanter cloud still wonder. Everyone had theories which to a greater or lesser extent conflicted with the story in court. Here is mine.

Nothing in the IRA's history suggests an overwhelming fear of killing innocent civilians, neither are its members suicidal martyrs in the Japanese or Islamic Fundamentalist tradition. The British expected a timed bomb to be driven in and set on Monday evening, and possibly even a blocking-car or some last-minute reconnaissance the day before. A reconnaissance would need at the most two people. To find all three in town on Sunday was a complete surprise, but, as in the old Chinese maxim, no military plan survives contact with the enemy. Over weeks or months the British had devised a plan for a move at the last moment, to catch bombers and their bomb together. The surveillance by this stage would need to be extremely thorough, but then, with the bomb already in Gibraltar and an arrest minutes away, the consequences of watchers being spotted by the bombers would hardly matter. They might make a run for the border and be cut off as they crossed the runway. But could anyone have expected to watch all three on the Sunday, watch them return to Spain, await their re-arrival on Monday? Operation Flavius does not seem to have prepared for that contingency; three bombers and no bomb is amateur behaviour. But how could the man who ran the operation trust that it would still work on the intended day? The bombers looked very 'surveillance-aware'. Perhaps they'd discovered they were being watched; perhaps they would abort the mission. An enormous effort, which had received the highest government sanction, would be thrown away. Whether the British believed the Renault contained a bomb or not, the three would have to be arrested in whatever meaning of the word. But if there was no bomb in Gibraltar, evidence for a trial would be thin.

So what really did happen in Gibraltar on 6 March? A case of mistaken belief? An operation that went wrong? A carefully created opportunity that was too good to miss? Today in Scotland, a new chant rises from the terraces of Glasgow Rangers football club: 'SAS, bang-bang-bang, SAS, bang-bang-bang.'

Douglas Celecia's photographs: The gun on the ground is a .38 Smith and Wesson, the gun of the Gibraltar police, and not a 9mm Browning, the gun of the SAS soldier.

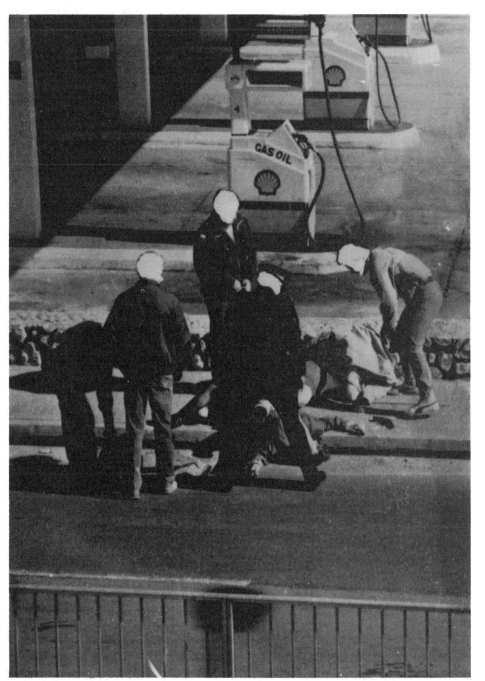

MARTIN AMIS
THE MURDEREE

This is a true story, but I can't believe it's really happening. It's a murder story, too. I can't believe my luck. This is the story of a murder. It hasn't happened yet. But it will. (It had better.) I know the murderer, I know the murderee. I know the time, I know the place. I know the motive, I know the means. I know who will be the foil, the fool, the poor foal, also utterly destroyed. And I couldn't stop them, I don't think, even if I wanted to. The girl will die. It's what she always wanted. You can't stop people, once they *start*. You can't stop people, once they *start creating*.

What a gift. It's a shame to take the money. Novelists don't usually have it this good, do they, when something true happens (something unified, dramatic and reasonably commercial), and they just write it down? What a gift from real life.

I must remain calm. I have my own deadline here, too, don't forget. Oh, the agitation. Someone is tickling my heart with muscular fingers. Death is much on people's minds. Everybody must keep their nerve.

Three days ago I flew in on a red-eye from New York. I practically had the airplane to myself and could stretch out on the great lumpen chesterfield, calling piteously to the stewardesses for pillows and cold water. But the red-eye did what a red-eye does. Look at them! Incarnadined . . . Shaken awake to a sticky bun at one-thirty in the morning, my time. I moved to a window-seat and watched through the bright mist the fields forming their regiments, in full parade order, like an army the size of England. Then the city itself, as taut and delicate as a cobweb. I had the airplane to myself because nobody in their right mind wants to go to Europe, not just now, not for the time being. America has had it with Europe. Everybody wants to come the other way, as Heathrow confirmed. It reeked of sleep, reeked of it, the whole complex. Somnopolis. There were hardly any Arrivals, apart from me; the business of the airport was all Departures. As I stood in some stalled passage and listened to the canned instructions I looked down on the lots and runways through the layered insult of dawn rain: all the sharks with their fins erect, threshers, baskers, great whites—killers, killers, killers every one.

As for the apartment—well, it takes my breath away. I mean it. When I come through the door I go *tee hee hee*. It cracks me up. The place kills me. All this for a personal ad in the *New York Review of Books*? I have certainly got the better of the deal. Yes, I have well and truly stiffed Mark Asprey. I tramp through these rooms and think with shame of my contorted little crib in Hell's Kitchen. The guy's a fellow writer, after all, and I would have felt happier, if not with exact equivalence, then with broad parity. Of course even I suspect that the décor is in doubtful taste. What does he write? Musicals? (He writes charming notes. 'Dear Sam: Welcome!' it begins.) Not a thing in the place is content to be merely handy or convenient. The toilet-brush is a moustachioed sceptre. The kitchen taps squirm with gargoyles. Here is someone who heats his morning coffee on the torched wind of Circassian dancing girls. Mr Asprey is a bachelor, that much is clear. For instance, there are a great many signed photographs on the walls—models, actresses. In this respect his bedroom is like some joint called Two Guys from Italy. But it isn't his pasta they're praising. The effortful inscription and looped signature, self-injury to the tender, the legendary throat.

On top of all this I get the use of his car, his A-to-B device, which obediently awaits me on the street. In his note he apologizes on its behalf, letting me know that he has a better one, moored to his country cottage. Yesterday I staggered out and took a look at it. Of the latest design, the car aspires to stone-grey invisibility. Even my scrutiny seemed to embarrass it. Features include fool-the-eye dent-marks, a removable toupee of rust on the hood and adhesive key scratches all over the paintwork. An English strategy: envy-pre-emption. Things have changed, things have remained the same, over the past ten years. No doubt there'll be surprises when I start to look around, but I always felt I knew where England was heading. America was the one you wanted to watch . . . I climbed in and took a spin around the block. I say *spin* to help account for the ten-minute dizzy spell that hit me when I came back into the apartment. I was impressed by its force. Giddiness and a new nausea, a moral nausea, coming from the gut (like waking from a disgraceful dream and looking with dread for the blood on your hands). On the front passenger seat, under the elegant rag of a white silk scarf, lies a heavy car-tool. Mark Asprey must be afraid of something. He must be afraid of London's poor.

Three days in and I am ready—I am ready to write. Real life is happening so fast that I can no longer delay. You know, I genuinely can't believe it. Twenty years of fastidious torment, twenty years of non-starting, and then: pow! Suddenly I'm ready. Let me say with all modesty and caution that I have the makings of a really snappy little thriller. Original, too. Not a whodunit. More a whydoit. I feel sickly and enraptured. I feel green. I think I am less a novelist than a queasy cleric, taking down the minutes of real life. Technically speaking, I am also, I suppose, an accessory before the fact, but to hell with all that for now. (I woke up today and thought, If London is a spider's web, then where do I fit in? Maybe I'm the fly. I'm the fly.) Hurry. I always assumed I'd start with the murderee, with her, with Nicola Six. But no, that isn't quite right. Let's start with the bad guy. Yeah. Keith. Let's start with the murderer.

The Murderer

Keith Talent was a bad guy. Keith Talent was a very bad guy. You might even say that he was the worst guy. But not *the* worst, not the very worst ever. There *were* worse guys. Where? There in the hot light of the Superette, for example, with car keys, beige singlet and a six-pack of Particular Brews, the scuffle at the door, the foul threat and the elbow in the black neck of the wailing lady, then the car with its rust and its waiting blonde, and off to do the next thing, whatever, whatever necessary. In the eyes, a tiny unsmiling universe. No. Keith wasn't *that* bad. He had saving graces. He didn't hate people for ready-made reasons. He was at least *multiracial* in outlook—thoughtlessly, helplessly so. Intimate encounters with strange-hued women had sweetened him somewhat. His saving graces all had names. What with the Fetnabs and Fatimas he had known, the Nketchis and Iqbalas, the Michikos and Boguslawas, the Ramsarwatees and Rajashwaris—Keith was, in this sense, a man of the world. These were the chinks in his coal-black armour. God bless them all.

Although he liked nearly everything else about himself, Keith hated his saving graces. In his view they constituted his only major shortcoming—his one tragic flaw. When the moment arrived, in the office by the loading bay at the plant off the M4 near Bristol, with his great face crammed into the prickling nylon, and the proud woman shaking her trembling head at him, and Chick Purchase and Dean Pleat both screaming *Do it! Do it* (he still remembered their meshed mouths writhing), Keith had definitely failed to do the biz. He had proved incapable of clubbing the Asian woman to her knees and of going on clubbing until the man in the uniform opened the safe. Why had he failed? Why, Keith, why? In truth he had felt far from well: half the night up some lane in a car full of burping criminals; no breakfast, no bowel movement; and now, to top it off, everywhere he looked he saw green grass, fresh trees, rolling hills. Chick Purchase, furthermore, had already crippled the second guard, and Dean Pleat soon vaulted back over the counter and self-righteously laid into the woman with his rifle butt. So Keith's qualms had changed nothing—except his career prospects in armed robbery. (It's tough at the top, and it's tough at the bottom, too; Keith's name was muck thereafter.) If he could have done it, he would have done it, joyfully. He just didn't have . . . he just didn't have the talent.

After that Keith turned his back on armed robbery once and for all. He took up racketeering. In London, broadly speaking, racketeering meant fighting about drugs; in the part of West London that Keith called home, racketeering meant fighting about drugs with black people. Villainy works through escalation, and escalation dominance: success goes to the men who can manage the exponential jump, to the men who can regularly *astonish* with their violence. It took Keith several crunchy beatings, and the first signs of a liking for hospital food, before he concluded that he wasn't cut out for racketeering. During one of his convalescences, when he spent a lot of time in the street cafés of Golborne Road, Keith grew preoccupied with a certain enigma. The enigma was this. How come you often saw black guys with white girls (always blondes, always, presumably for maximum contrast-gain), and never saw white guys with black girls? Did the black guys beat up the white guys who went out with black girls? No, or not much; you had to be discreet, though, and in his experience lasting relationships were seldom formed. Then how was it done? It came to him in a flash of inspiration. The black guys beat up the black *girls* who went out with the white guys! Of course. So much simpler. He pondered the wisdom of this and drew a lesson from it, a lesson which, in his heart, he had long understood. If you're going to be violent, stick to women. Stick to the weak. Keith gave up racketeering. He turned over a new leaf. Having renounced violent crime, Keith prospered, and rose steadily towards the very crest of his new profession: non-violent crime.

Keith worked as a *cheat*. There he stands on the street corner, with three or four colleagues, with three or four fellow *cheats*; they laugh and cough (they're always coughing) and flap their arms for warmth; they look like terrible birds . . . On good days he rose early and put in long hours, going out into the world, into society, with the intention of cheating it. Keith cheated people with his limousine service at airports and train stations; he cheated people with his fake scents and colognes at the pavement stalls of Oxford Street and Bishopsgate (his two main lines were Scandal and Outrage); he cheated people with non-pornographic pornography in the back rooms of short-lease stores; and he cheated people on the street everywhere with the upturned cardboard box or milk crate and the three warped playing-cards: Find the Lady! Here, often, and occasionally elsewhere, the boundaries between violent crime and its non-violent little brother were hard to descry. Keith earned three times as much as the Prime Minister and never had any money, losing heavily every day in the turf accountants on the Portobello Road. He never won. Sometimes he would ponder this, on alternate Thursday lunchtimes, in sheepskin overcoat, his head bent over the racing page, as he queued for his unemployment benefit, and then drove to the turf accountants on the Portobello Road. So Keith's life might have elapsed over the years. He never had what it took to be a murderer, not on his own. He needed his murderee. The foreigners, the checked and dog-toothed Americans, the leering lens-faced Japanese, standing stiff over the cardboard box or the milk crate—they never found the lady. But *Keith* did. Keith found her.

Of course, he already had a lady, little Kath, who had recently presented him with a child. By and large Keith had welcomed the pregnancy: it was, he liked to joke, quite a handy new way of putting the wife in hospital. He had decided that the baby, when it came, would be called Keith—Keith Jr. Kath, remarkably, had other ideas. Yet Keith was inflexible, wavering only once, when he briefly entertained the idea of calling the baby Clive, after his dog, a large, elderly and unpredictable Alsatian. He changed his mind once more; Keith it was to be, then . . . Swaddled in blue, the baby came home, with mother. Keith personally helped them from the ambulance. As Kath started on the dishes, Keith sat by the stolen fire and frowned at the new arrival. There was something wrong with the baby, something seriously wrong. The trouble with the baby was that the baby was a girl. Keith looked deep into himself, and rallied. 'Keithette,' Kath heard him murmur, as her knees settled on the cold lino. 'Keithene. Keitha. Keithinia.'

'No, Keith,' she said.

'Keithnab,' said Keith, with an air of slow discovery. 'Nkeithi.'

'No, Keith.'

After a few days, whenever Kath cautiously addressed the baby as 'Kim', Keith no longer swore at his wife or slammed her up against the wall with any conviction. 'Kim', after all, was the name of one of Keith's heroes, one of Keith's gods. And Keith was cheating hard that week, cheating on everyone, it seemed, and especially his wife. So Kim Talent it was—Kim Talent, little Kim.

The man had ambition. Tenderly he nursed his hopes and his dreams. Keith had no intention, or no desire, to be a *cheat* for the rest of his life. Even he found the work demoralizing. And mere cheating would never get him the things he wanted, the goods and services he wanted, not while a series of decisive wins at the turf accountants continued to elude him. He sensed that Keith Talent had been put here for something a little bit special. To be fair, it must be said that murder was not in his mind, not yet, except perhaps in some ghostly *potentia* that precedes all thought and action . . . Character is destiny. Keith had often been told, by various magistrates, girl-friends and probation officers, that he had a 'poor character', and he had always fondly owned up to the fact. But did that mean he had a poor destiny? Not on your life. Waking early, perhaps, as Kath clumsily dragged herself from the bed to attend to little Kim, or wedged in one of the traffic jams that routinely enchained his day, Keith would mentally pursue an alternative vision, one of wealth, fame and a kind of spangled super-legitimacy—the chrome spokes of a possible future in World Darts.

A casual darter or arrowman all his life, right back to the bald board on the kitchen door, Keith had recently got serious. He'd always thrown for his pub, of course, and followed the sport: you could almost hear sacred music when, on those special nights (three or four times a week), Keith laid out the cigarettes on the arm of the couch and prepared to watch darts on television. But now he had designs on the other side of the screen. To his own elaborately concealed astonishment, Keith found himself in the Last Sixteen of the Sparrow Masters, an annual inter-pub competition which he had nonchalantly entered some months ago, on the advice of various friends and admirers. At the end of that road there basked the contingency of a televised final, a £5,000 cheque, and a play-off, also televised, with his hero and darting model, the world number one, Kim Twemlow. After that, well, after that, the rest was television.

And television was all about everything he did not have and was full of all the people he did not know and could never be. Television was the great shop-front, lightly electrified, up against which Keith crushed his nose. And now among the squirming motes, the impossible prizes, he saw a doorway, or an arrow, or a beckoning hand (with a dart in it), and everything said—Darts. Pro-Darts. World Darts. He's down there in his garage, putting in the hours, his eyes still stinging from the ineffable, the heart-breaking beauty of a brand-new dartboard, stolen that very day.

Keith didn't look like a murderer. He looked like a murderer's dog. (No disrespect to Keith's dog Clive, who had signed on well before the fact, and whom Keith didn't in the least resemble anyway.) Keith looked like a murderer's dog, eager familiar of ripper or body-snatcher or grave-stalker. His eyes held a strange radiance—for a moment it reminded you of health, health hidden or sleeping or otherwise mysteriously absent. Though frequently bloodshot, the eyes seemed to pierce. In fact the light sprang off them. And it wasn't at all pleasant or encouraging, this one-way splendour. His eyes were television. The face itself was leonine, puffy with hungers and as dry as soft fur. Keith's crowning glory, his hair, was thick and full-bodied; but it always had the look of being recently washed, imperfectly rinsed, and then, still slick with cheap shampoo, slow-dried in a huddled pub—the thermals of the booze, the sallowing fag-smoke. Those eyes, and their urban severity . . . Like the desolating gaiety of a fundless paediatric hospital (Welcome to the Peter Pan Ward), or like a criminal's cream Rolls-Royce, parked at dusk between a tube station and a flower stall, the eyes of Keith Talent shone with tremendous accommodations made to money. And murder? The eyes—was there enough blood in them for *that*? Not now, not yet. He had the talent, somewhere, but he would need the murderee to bring it out. Soon, he would find the lady.

Or she would find him.

C*hick* Purchase. I know—it's funny, isn't it. A contraction of Charles. In America it's Chuck. In England it's *Chick*. Some name. Some country.

Powerfully relieved about the first chapter, though I don't dare re-read it yet. I wonder if I ever will. For reasons not yet altogether clear, I seem to have adopted a jovial and lordly tone. It feels anachronistic, but appropriate. Careful. Remember: Keith is modern, modern, modern. And soon I must face the murderee.

It would be nice to expatiate on how good it feels, after all these years, to sit down and start writing a novel. But let's not get any big ideas. This isn't fiction. This is really happening.

How do I know, for instance, that Keith works as a *cheat*? Because he tried to *cheat* me, on the way in from Heathrow. I'd been standing under the sign saying TAXIS for about half an hour when the royal-blue Cavalier made its second circuit and pulled up at the bay. Out he climbed.

'Taxi, sir?' he said, and briskly picked up my bag.

'You're not a taxi.'

'You won't get a cab here, pal. No way.'

I asked him how much. He named an outlandish sum.

'Limo, innit,' he explained.

'That's not a limo. It's just a car.'

'Just what's on the meter, yeah?' he said, but I was already climbing into the back seat and was fast asleep before we pulled away.

I awoke some time later. We were approaching Slough, and the meter said £54.50.

'Slough!'

His eyes were warily burning at me in the rear-view mirror.

'Wait a second, wait a second,' I began. One thing about my illness: I've never been braver. 'Look. I know my way around. I'm not over here to see Harrods and Buckingham Palace. I don't say *twenty quids* and *Trafaljar Square*. Slough? Christ! If this is a kidnap or a murder, then OK. Otherwise, take me to London for thirty-five pounds.'

He pulled up, unhurriedly. Yawn, I thought: this really is a murder. He turned his head and showed me a confiding sneer.

'What it is,' he said, 'what it is—I seen you was asleep. I thought: "He's asleep. Looks as though he could use it. I know. I'll pop in on me mum." Never mind that,' he said, jerking his head in brutal dismissal towards the clock, which was of curious design and possibly home manufacture and now said £63.80. 'Don't mind, do you, pal?' He pointed to a line of pebble-dash semis—we were, I now saw, in some kind of dormitory estate, green, shopless. 'She's sick, see. Won't be five minutes. OK?'

'What's that?' I said. I referred to the sounds coming from the car stereo, solid thunks followed by shouted numbers against a savage background of whoops and screams.

'Darts,' he said, and switched it off. 'I'd ask you in but—me old mum. Here. Have a read of this.'

So I sat in the back of the Cavalier while my driver went to see his mum. Actually he was doing nothing of the kind. What he was doing (as he would later proudly confide) was wheelbarrowing a lightly clad Analiese Furnish around the living-room while her current protector, who worked nights, slept with his usual soundness in the room above . . .

I held in my hands a four-page brochure, pressed on me by the murderer (though of course he wasn't a murderer yet. He had a way to go). On the back was a colour photograph of the Queen and a crudely superimposed perfume bottle: '"Outrage"—by Ambrosio.' On the front was a black-and-white photograph of my chauffeur, smiling unreliably. 'KEITH TALENT,' it said:

* ★ Chauffeur and courier services
* ★ Own limousine
* ★ Casino consultant
* ★ Luxury goods and Celebrity purchases
* ★ Darts lessons given
* ★ London operative for Ambrosio of Milan,
  Perfumes and Furs

There followed some more information about the perfumes, 'Scandal', 'Outrage', and minor lines called Mirage, Disguise, Duplicity and Sting, and beneath, in double quotes, accompanied by an address and telephone number, with misplaced apostrophes: Keith's the Name, Scent's the Game. The two middle pages of the brochure were blank. I folded it into my middle pocket, quite idly; but it has since proved very valuable to me.

With sloping gait and two casual corrections of the belt, Keith came down the garden path.

There was £143.10 on the blatting clock when the car pulled up and I awoke again.

'Home sweet home,' said Keith.

Slowly I climbed from the car's slept-in, trailer smell, as if from a second aircraft, and unbent myself in front of the house—and the house massive, like an ancient terminal.

Keith paused with a flinch as he lifted my bag from the trunk. 'It's a church,' he said wonderingly.

'It used to be a rectory or a vicarage or something.' I pointed to an engraving on the other wall, high up: 'Anno Domini 1876.'

'1876!' he said. 'Some vicar had all this . . .'

Making no small display of the courtesy, Keith carried my bag in through the fenced front garden and stood there while I got my keys from the lady on the ground floor. I turned. At the other end of the street, some distance away, you could see a motorcade and the drab of camouflage vehicles, and you could hear the roll and clatter, the sound of thunderous rearrangements.

'What's happening?'

Keith shrugged in resigned ignorance. 'All cloaked in secrecy, innit.'

We entered through a second front door and climbed a broad flight of stairs. I think we were about equally impressed by the opulence and elaboration of the apartment. This is some joint, I have to admit. After a few weeks here even the great Presley would have started to pine for all the elegance and simplicity of Graceland. Keith cast his bright glance around the place with a looter's cruel yet professional eye. For the second time that morning I nonchalantly reviewed the possibility that I was about to be murdered. Keith would be out of here ten minutes later, my flight-bag over his shoulder, lumpy with appurtenances. Instead he asked me who owned the place and what he did.

I told him.

Keith looked sceptical. This just wasn't right.

'Mostly for theatre and television,' I said.

Now all was clear. 'TV?' he said coolly.

For some reason I added, 'I'm in TV too.'

Keith nodded, much enlightened. Somewhat chastened also; and I have to say it touched me, this chastened look. Of course (he was thinking), TV people all know each other and fly to and from the great cities and borrow each other's flats. Common sense. Yes, behind all the surface activity of Keith's eyes there formed the vision of a heavenly elite, cross-hatching the troposphere like satellite TV—above it, above it all.

'Yeah, well I'm due to appear on TV myself. Hopefully. In a month or two. Darts.'

'Darts?'

'Darts.'

And then it began. He stayed for three and a half hours. People are amazing, aren't they? They'll tell you everything if you give them time. And I have always been a good listener. I have always been a talented listener. I really do want to hear it—I don't know why. Of course at that stage I was perfectly disinterested; I had no idea what was happening, what was forming right in front of me. Within fifteen minutes I was being told, in shocking detail, about Analiese—and Iqbala, and Trish, and Debbee. Laconic but unabashed mentions of wife and daughter. And then all that painful stuff about violent crime and Chick Purchase. True, I gave him a fair amount to drink: beer, or lager, plentifully heaped like bombs on their racks in Mark Asprey's refrigerator. In the end he charged me twenty-five pounds for the ride (special TV rate, perhaps) and gave me a ball-point pen shaped like a dart, with which I now write these words. He also told me that he could be found, every lunchtime and every evening, in a pub called the Black Cross on the Portobello Road.

I would find him there, right enough. And so would the lady.

When Keith left I sacked out immediately. Not that I had much say in the matter. Twenty-two hours later I opened my eyes again and was greeted by a strange and distressing sight. Myself, on the ceiling mirror. (I thought the drawing-room was brothel-opulent; the bedroom is outright sex-athletic, all leather and glaze.) I looked—I looked not well, staked out there on the satin. I seemed to be pleading, pleading with me, myself. Dr Slizard tells me that I have about three months more of this to get through, and then everything will change.

I have been out and about a bit since then; yes, I have made several tremulous sorties. So far, it doesn't seem as bad as some people say. Ten years I've been gone, and what's been happening? Ten more years of Relative Decline . . . I'm now well in with Keith Talent. I think I cultivated him in the first place as a kind of preparation for the streets of London. I am also ingratiating myself with our third party, the fool or foil, the poor foal: Guy Clinch. But none of this would ever have got started without the girl. It didn't have a hope in hell without the girl. She was the absolute *donnée*. I suppose that instant in the Black Cross set the whole story in motion. And now Nicola Six is taking things into her own hands.

The English, Lord love them, they still talk about the weather.

Yet suddenly the weather is well worth talking about. It's not just something that makes you hang your head and say, *Christ . . .* The weather is super-atmospheric and therefore, in a sense, super-meteorological (can you really call it *weather*?). But the reasons for it are apparently well understood. It will go on for the rest of the summer, they say. I approve, with one qualification: it's picked the wrong year to happen in. The weather, if we can still call it that, is frequently very beautiful, but it frightens me, as indeed does everything now.

The Murderee

The black cab will move away, irrecoverably and for ever, its driver paid, and handsomely tipped, by the murderee. She will walk down the dead-end street. The heavy car will be waiting; its lights will come on as it lumbers towards her. It will stop, and idle, as the passenger door swings open.

His face will be barred in darkness, but she will see shattered glass on the passenger seat and the car-tool ready on his lap.

'Get in.'

She will lean forward. 'You,' she will say, in intense recognition: 'Yes, *you.*'

'Get *in.*'

And in she'll climb . . .

What is this destiny or condition (and perhaps, like the look of the word's ending, it tends towards the feminine: a feminine ending), what *is* it, what does it mean, to be a murderee?

In the case of Nicola Six, tall, dark, and thirty-four, it was bound up with a delusion, lifelong, and not in itself unmanageable. Right from the start, from the moment that her thoughts began to be consecutive, Nicola knew two strange things. The second strange thing was that she must never tell anyone about the first strange thing. The first strange thing was this: she always knew what was going to happen next. Not all the time (the gift was not obsessively consulted), and not every little thing; but she always knew what was going to happen next. Right from the start she had a friend—Enola, Enola Gay. Enola wasn't real. Enola came from inside the head of Nicola Six. Nicola was an only child and knew she always would be.

You can imagine how things might work out. Nicola is seven years old, for instance, and her parents are taking her on a picnic, with another family: why, pretty Dominique will be there, a friend, perhaps, a living friend for the only child. But little Nicola, immersed in romantic thoughts and perfectly happy with Enola, doesn't want to come along (watch how she screams and grips!). She doesn't want to come along because she knows that the afternoon will end in disaster, in blood and iodine and tears. And so it proves. A hundred yards from the grown-ups (so impenetrably arrayed round the square sheet in the sunshine), Nicola stands on the crest of a slope with her new friend, pretty Dominique. And of course Nicola knows what is going to happen next: the girl will hesitate or stumble: reaching out to steady her, Nicola will accidentally propel her playmate downwards, down into the rocks and the briers. She will then have to run and shout, and drive in silence somewhere, and sit on the hospital bench swinging her feet and listlessly asking for ice-cream. And so it proves. On television at the age of four she saw the first warnings (thermal pulse, blast wave) and the circles of concentric devastation, with London like a bull's-eye in the centre of the board. She knew that would happen, too. It was just a matter of time.

When Nicola was good she was very very good. But when she was bad . . . About her parents she had no feelings one way or the other: this was her silent, inner secret. They both died, anyway, together, as she had always known they would. So why hate them? So why love them? After she got the call she drove reflexively to the airport. The car itself was like a tunnel of cold wind. An airline official showed her into the VIP lounge: it contained a bar, and forty or fifty people in varying degrees of distress. She drank the brandy pressed on her by the steward. 'Free,' he said. A television was wheeled in. And then, incredibly (even Nicola was consternated), they showed live film of the scattered wreckage, and the body-bags lined up on the fields of France. In the VIP lounge there were scenes of protest and violent rejection. One old man kept distractedly offering money to a uniformed PR officer. Coldly Nicola drank more brandy, wondering how death could take people so unprepared. That night she had acrobatic sex with some vile pilot. She was nineteen by this time, and had long left home. Potently, magically, uncontrollably attractive, Nicola was not yet beautiful. But already she was an ill wind, blowing no good.

Considered more generally—when you looked at the human wreckage she left in her slipstream, the nervous collapses, the shattered careers, the suicide bids, the blighted marriages (and rottener divorces)—Nicola's knack of reading the future left her with one or two firm assurances: that no one would ever love her enough, and those that did were not worth being loved enough by. The typical Nicola romance would end, near the doorway of her attic flat, with the man of the moment sprinting down the passage, his trousers round his knees, a ripped jacket thrown over his ripped shirt, and hotly followed by Nicola herself (now in a night-dress, now in underwear, now naked beneath a half-furled towel), either to speed him on his way with a blood libel and a skilfully hurled ashtray, or else to win back his love, by apologies, by caresses, or by main force. In any event the man of the moment invariably kept going. Often she would fly right out into the street. On several occasions she had taken a brick to the waiting car. On several more she had lain down in front of it. All this changed nothing, of course. The car would always leave at the highest speed of which it was mechanically capable, though sometimes, admittedly, in reverse gear. Back in the flat, staunching her wrists, perhaps, or pressing an ice-cube to her lip (or a lump of meat to her eye), Nicola would look at herself in the mirror, would look at what remained and think how strange—how strange, that she had been right all along. She knew it would end like this. And so it proved. The diary she sometimes kept was therefore just the chronicle of a death foretold . . .

One of those people who should never drink anything at all, Nicola drank a very great deal. But it depended. One or two mornings a month, stiff with pride, deafened with aspirin (and reckless with Bloody Marys), Nicola would adumbrate serious reform: for example, only two colossal cocktails before dinner, a broad maximum of half a bottle of wine with her meal, and then just the one whisky or *digestif* before bedtime. She would frequently stick to the new regime right up to and certainly including the whisky or *digestif* before bedtime the following day. By then, bedtime looked a long way off. There was always a lot of shouting and fist-fighting to do before bedtime. And what about *after* bedtime, or after the *first* bedtime, with several bouts of one thing or the other still to go? So she always failed. She could see herself failing (there she was, clearly failing), and so she failed. Did Nicola Six drink alone? Yes, she drank alone. You *bet*. And why did she drink alone? Because she was alone. And she was alone, now, at night, more than formerly. What could never be endured, it turned out, was the last swathe of time before sleep came, the path from larger day to huger night, a little death when the mind was still alive and kicking. Thus the glass banged down on the round table; the supposedly odourless ashtray gave its last weak swirl; and then the baby-walk, the smudged trend to the loathed bedding. That was how it had to end.

The other ending, the real death, the last thing that already existed in the future was now growing in size as she moved forward to confront or greet it. Where would she see the murderer, where would she find him—in the park, the library, in the sad café, or walking past her in the street half-naked with a plank over his shoulder? The murder had a place, and a date, even a time: some minutes after midnight, on her thirty-fifth birthday. Nicola would click through the darkness of the dead-end street. Then the car, the grunt of its brakes, the door swinging open and the murderer (his face in shadow, the car-tool on his lap, one hand extended to seize her hair) saying *Get in. Get in* . . . And in she climbed.

It was fixed. It was written. The murderer was not yet a murderer. But the murderee had always been a murderee.

Where would she find him, how would she dream him, when would she summon him? On the important morning she awoke wet with the usual nightmares. She went straight to her bath and lay there for a long time, round-eyed, with her hair pinned up. On important days she always felt herself to be the object of scrutiny, lewd and furious scrutiny. Her head now looked small or telescoped, set against the squirming refractions of the giantness beneath the water. She rose with dramatic suddenness from the bath and paused before reaching for the towel. Then she stood naked in the middle of the warm room protectively oiling her breasts and thinking about pornography.

The funeral, the cremation she was due to attend that day was not a significant one. Nicola Six, who hardly knew or remembered the dead woman, had been obliged to put in a tedious half an hour on the telephone before she managed to get herself asked along. The dead woman had briefly employed Nicola in her antique shop, years ago. For a month or two the murderee had sat smoking cigarettes in the zestless grotto off Fulham Broadway. Then she had stopped doing that. This was always the way with Nicola's more recent jobs, of which there had, for a while, been a fair number. She did the job, and then, after an escalating and finally overlapping series of late mornings, four-hour lunches, and early departures, she was considered to have *let everyone down* (she wasn't there ever), and stopped going in. Nicola always knew when this moment had come, and chose that day to stop going in. The fact that Nicola knew things would end that way lent great tension to each job she took, right from the first week, the first day, the first morning . . . In the more distant past she had worked as a publisher's reader, a cocktail waitress, a telephonist, a croupier, a tourist operative, a model, a librarian, a kissogram girl, an archivist, and an actress. An actress—she had got quite far with that. In her early twenties she had done rep, Royal Shakespeare, panto, a few television plays. She still had a trunk full of outfits and some videotapes (poor little rich girl, spry newly-wed, naked houri maddeningly glimpsed through fog-smoke and veils). Acting was therapeutic, though dramatic roles confused her further. She was happiest with comedy, farce, custard-pie. The steadiest time of her adult life had been the year in Brighton, taking the lead in *Jack and the Beanstalk*. Playing a man seemed to help. She did Jack in short blazer and black tights, and with her hair down. A million mothers wondered why their sons came home so green and feverish, and crept burdened to bed without their suppers. But then the acting bit of her lost its moorings and drifted out into real life.

With a towel round her belly she sat before the mirror, itself a theatrical memento, with its proscenium of brutal bulbs. Again she felt unfriendly eyes playing on her back. She went at her face like an artist, funeral colours, black, beige, blood red. Rising, she turned to the bed and reviewed her burial clothes and their unqualified sable. Even her elaborate underwear was black; even the clips on her garter belt were black, black. She opened her wardrobe, releasing the full-length mirror, and stood sideways with a hand flat on her stomach, feeling everything that a woman would hope to feel at such a moment. As she sat on the bed and tipped herself backwards for the first black stocking, mind-body memories took her back to earlier ablutions, self-inspections, intimate preparations. A weekend out of town with some new man of the moment. As she sat in the car on the Friday afternoon, after the heavy lunch, as they dragged through Swiss Cottage to the motorway, or through the curling systems of Clapham and Brixton and beyond (where London seems unwilling ever to relinquish the land, wants to squat on those fields right up to the rocks and the cliffs and the water), Nicola would feel a pressure in those best panties of hers, as it were the opposite of sex, like the stirring of new hymen being prettily and pinkly formed. By the time they reached Totteridge or Tooting, Nicola was a virgin again. With what perplexity would she turn to the voluble disappointment, the babbling mistake at her side with his hands on the wheel. After a glimpse of the trees in the dusk, a sodden church, a dumbfounded sheep, Nicola would drink little at the hotel or the borrowed cottage and would sleep inviolate with her hands crossed over her heart like a saint. Sulky in slumber, the man of the moment would nevertheless awake to find that practically half his entire torso was inside Nicola's mouth; and Saturday lunchtime was always a debauch on every front. She hardly ever made it to Sunday. The weekend would end that evening: a stunned and wordless return down the motorway, a single-passenger mini-cab drive of ghostly length and costliness, or Nicola Six standing alone on a dismal railway platform, erect and unblinking, with a suitcase full of shoes.

But let us be clear about this: she had great powers—great powers. All women whose faces and bodies more or less neatly fill the contemporary mould have some notion of these privileges and magics. During their pomp and optimum, however brief and relative, they occupy the erotic centre. Some feel lost, some surrounded or crowded, but there they are, in a China-sized woodland of rock-hard phallus. With Nicola Six the gender worship (or pimple yearning, to put it at its lowest) was translated, was fantastically heightened: it was available in the form of human love. She had the power of inspiring love, almost anywhere. Forget about making strong men weep. Seven-stone pacifists shouldered their way through street riots to be home in case she called. Family men abandoned sick children to wait in the rain outside her flat. Semi-literate builders and bankers sent her sonnet sequences. She pauperized gigolos, she spayed studs, she hospitalized heart-breakers. They were never the same again; they lost their heads. And the thing with her (what *was* it with her), the thing with her was that she had to receive this love and send it back in opposite form, not just cancelled but murdered. Character is destiny; and Nicola knew where her destiny lay.

Fifteen minutes later, dressed for death, she called her black cab and drank two cups of black coffee and tasted with hunger the black tobacco of a French cigarette.

In Golders Green she dismissed the taxi, and it pulled away for ever. She knew she would get a lift back: you always did, from funerals. The sky above the red-brick lodge she entered was certainly dull enough for a person to take leave of it with decency. As usual she was quite late, but the volley of pale glances did not pierce her. With no attempt at self-muffling she walked evenly to the back and slipped into an empty aisle, of which there was no shortage. The dead woman was not being populously farewelled. So this was all you got: zooty sideburns and masturbator's pallor of an old ted in a black suit, and the secular obsequies. Nicola longed equally for a cigarette and the lines you sometimes heard: a short time to live, full of misery. She was always especially stirred—this was why she came—by the spectacle of the bereaved elderly, particularly the women. The poor sheep, the dumbfounded sheep (even mere nature dumbfounds them), as reliable as professional mourners but too good at it really, too passionate, with hair like feather dusters, and frailly convulsed with brute grief, the selfish terrors . . . Nicola yawned. Everything around her said school, the busts and plaques, and all the panels with their use of wood to quell and dampen. She hardly noticed the discreet trundling of the coffin, knowing it was empty and the body already vaporized by fire.

Afterwards, in the Dispersal Area (a heavy blackbird was flying low and at an angle over the sopping grass), Nicola Six, looking and sounding very very good, explained to various interested parties who she was and what she was doing there. It solaced the old to see such piety in the relatively young. She reviewed the company with eyes of premonitory inquiry, and with small inner shrugs of disappointment. In the car-park she was offered several lifts; she accepted one more or less at random.

The driver, who was the dead woman's brother's brother-in-law, dropped her off on the Portobello Road, as instructed. Prettily Nicola said her goodbyes to him and his family, extending a gloved hand and receiving their thanks and praise for her attendance. She could hear them long after the car had pulled away, as she stood on the street readjusting her veil. Such a nice girl. So good of her to come. That skin! What hair! All the way back Nicola had been thinking how good a cigarette would look, white and round between her black fingers. But she was out of cigarettes, having almost gassed herself with tobacco on the way to Golders Green. She now progressed along the Portobello Road, and saw a pub whose name she took a liking to. 'TV AND DARTS' was the further recommendation of a painted sign on its door, to which a piece of cardboard had been affixed, saying 'AND PIMBALL'. All the skies of London seemed to be gathering directly overhead, with thunder ready to drop its plunger . . .

She entered the Black Cross. She entered the pub and its murk. She felt the place skip a beat as the door closed behind her, but she had been expecting that. Indeed, it would be a bad day (and that day would never come) when she entered a men's room, a teeming toilet such as this and turned no heads, caused no groans or whispers. She walked straight to the bar, lifed her veil with both hands, like a bride, surveyed the main actors of the scene, and immediately she knew, with pain, with gravid arrest, with intense recognition, that she had found him, her murderer.

When at last she returned to the flat Nicola laid out her diaries on the round table. She made an entry, unusually crisp and detailed: the final entry. The notebooks she used were Italian, their covers embellished with Latin script . . .

Now they had served their purpose and she wondered how to dispose of them. The story wasn't over, but the life was. She stacked the books and reached for a ribbon. The time had come for them to be put down.

Montherlant or somebody said that happiness writes white: it doesn't show up on the page. We all know this. The letter with the foreign postmark that tells of good weather, pleasant food and comfortable accommodation isn't nearly as much fun to read, or to write, as the letter that tells of rotting chalets, dysentery and drizzle. Who else but Tolstoy has made happiness really swing on the page? When I take on Chapter Three, when I take on Guy Clinch, I'll have to do, well, not happiness, but goodness, anyway. It's going to be rough.

The moment that Keith Talent saw Nicola Six—he dropped his third dart. Being a dart, a little missile of plastic and tungsten, it combined with gravity and efficiently plunged towards the centre of the earth. What halted its progress was Keith's left foot, which was protected only by the frayed canvas of a cheap running-shoe. The dart hurt, and drew a little bull's-eye of blood . . . I thought I might be able to make a nice play on words here. Cupid's dart, or something like that. Arrows of desire? But it wasn't desire that Nicola Six aroused in Keith Talent. Not primarily. I would say that greed and fear came first. Going for broke at the pinball table, Guy Clinch froze in mid-flail: you could hear the ball scuttling into the gutter. Then silence.

While the scene developed I melted, as they say, into the background. Of course I had no idea what was taking shape in front of me. No idea? Well, an inkling, maybe. This moment in the public house, this pub moment, I'm going to have to keep on coming back to it. Edging down the bar, I was intrigued only in the civilian sense—but powerfully intrigued. Every pub had its superstar, its hero, its pub athlete, and Keith was the Knight of the Black Cross: he *had* to step forward to deal with the royal tourist. He had to do it for the guys: for Wayne, Dean, Duane, for Norvis, Shakespeare, Bid Dread, for Godfrey the barman, for Fucker Burke, for Basim and Manjeet, for Bogdan, Majcek, Zbigniew.

Keith acted in the name of masculinity. He acted also, of course, in the name of *class*. Class! Yes, it's still here. Terrific staying power, and against all the historical odds. What *is* it with that old, *old* crap? The class system just doesn't know when to quit. Even a nuclear holocaust, I think, would fail to make that much of a dent in it. Crawling through the iodized shithouse that used to be England, people would still be brooding about accents and cocked pinkies, about maiden names and *settee* or *sofa*, about the proper way to eat a roach in society. Come on. Do you take the head off first, or start with the legs? Class never bothered Keith; he never thought about it 'as such'; part of a bygone era, whatever that was, class never worried him. It would surprise Keith a lot if you told him it was *class* that poisoned his every waking moment. At any rate, subliminally or otherwise, it was class that made Keith enlist a third actor in his dealings with Nicola Six. It was class that made Keith enlist Guy Clinch. Or maybe the murderee did it. Maybe she needed him. Maybe they both needed him, as a kind of fuel.

Do *I* need him? Yes. Evidently. Guy pressed himself on me, same as the other two. Now I must further ingratiate myself with all three. You've got to stop having any grand ideas. You're not in control, you can't pick and choose. This isn't fiction. Christ—this is really happening.

I left the Black Cross around four. It was my third visit. I needed the company, hair-raising though much of it was, and I was doing all right there, under Keith's wing. He introduced me to the Polacks and the brothers, or paraded me in front of them. He gave me a game of pool. He showed me how to cheat the fruit machine. I bought a lot of drinks, and took a lot of savage cajolery for my orange juices, my sodas, my cokes. Taking my life in my hands, I ate a pork pie. Only one real fight so far. An incredible flurry of fists and nuttings; it ended with Keith carefully kicking selected areas of a fallen figure wedged into the doorway to the Gents; Keith then returned to the bar, took a pull of beer, and returned to kick some more. It transpired that the culprit had been messing with Dean's darts. After the ambulance came and went Keith calmed down. 'Not with a man's darts,' Keith kept saying almost tearfully, shaking his head. People were bringing him brandies. 'You don't . . . not with his darts.'

I left the Black Cross around four. I went back to the apartment. I sat at the desk in Mark Asprey's bay-windowed office or study or library. Actually it's more like a trophy room. Actually the whole damn place is a trophy room. Walking from living-room to bedroom—and I'm thinking of the signed photographs, the erotic prints—you wonder why he didn't just nail a galaxy of G-strings to the walls. In here it's different. Here you're surrounded by cups and sashes, Tonis and Guggies, by framed presentations, commendations. Cherished and valued alike by the critical establishment, the media, and the world of academe, Mark Asprey has honorary degrees, pasteboard hats, three separate gowns from Oxford, Cambridge, Trinity College, Dublin. I must look at his books, of which there are a great many, in a great many editions, in a great many languages. Hungarian. Portuguese.

I left the Black Cross around four. I went back to the apartment. I sat there wondering why I just can't do it, why I just can't write, why I just can't *make anything up*. Then I saw her.

Across the way from Mark Asprey's bay-windowed library there is a lot-sized square of green, with two thin beds of flowers (low-ranking flowers, NUPE flowers) and a wooden bench where old-timers sometimes sit and seem to flicker in the wind. On this green patch, rather regrettably, rather disappointingly (how come Asprey stands for it?), there is also· a garbage tip: nothing outrageous, no compost or abandoned bath-tubs, just selected refuse, magazines, old toys, a running shoe, a kettle. This is a London theme; the attempt at greenery would itself appear to attract the trash. The cylinders of wire-netting they put up to protect young trees sufficiently resemble a container of some kind, so people cram them with beer cans, used tissues, yesterday's newspapers. In times of mass disorientation and anxiety . . . But we can get back to that. On with the story. The girl was there: Nicola, the murderee.

I was sitting at Mark Asprey's vast desk—I think I might even have been wringing my hands. Oh Lord, these chains! Something I have suffered for twenty years, the massive disappointment of *not writing*—perhaps exacerbated (I admit to the possibility) by Mark Asprey's graphic and plentiful successes in the sphere. It shocked my heart to see her: a soft blow to the heart, from within. Still wearing her funeral robes, the hat, the veil. In her black-gloved hands she held something solid, ribboned in red, the load settled on her hip and held close as if for comfort, like a child. Then she raised the veil and showed her face. She looked so . . . dramatic. She looked like the vamp in the ad, just before the asshole in the helicopter or the submarine shows up with the bath-oil or the chocolates. Could she see me, with that low sun behind her? I couldn't tell, but I thought: Nicola would know. She would know all about how light works on windows. She would know what you could get away with in the curtainless room, what adulteries, what fantastic betrayals . . .

Nicola turned, wavered, and steadied herself. She dropped her burden into the trash and, embracing her shoulders with crossed hands, moved off in a hurrying walk.

For perhaps five minutes of stretched time I waited. Then down I went and picked up my gift. Not knowing what I had, I sat on the bench and pulled the ribbon's knot. An adorably fat and feminine hand, chaos, a glittering intelligence. It made me blush with pornographic guilt. When I looked up I saw half of Nicola Six, thirty feet away, split by a young tree-trunk, not hiding but staring. Her stare contained—only clarity, great clarity. I gestured, as if to return what I held in my hands. But after a pulse of time she was walking off fast under the wrung hands of the trees.

I wish I could do Keith's voice. The *t*'s are viciously stressed. A brief guttural pop, like the first nanosecond of a cough or a hawk, accompanies the hard *k*. When he says *chaotic*, and he says it frequently, it sounds like a death-rattle. 'Month' comes out as *mumf*. He sometimes says, 'Im feory . . .', when he speaks theoretically. 'There' sounds like *dare* or *lair*. You could often run away with the impression that Keith Talent is eighteen months old.

In fact I've had to watch it with my characters' ages. I thought Guy Clinch was about twenty-seven. He is thirty-five. I thought Keith Talent was about forty-two. He is twenty-nine. I thought Nicola Six . . . No, I always knew what she was. Nicola Six is thirty-four. I fear for them, my youngers.

And meanwhile time goes about its immemorial work of

making everyone look and feel like shit. You got that? And meanwhile time goes about its immemorial work of making everyone look, and feel, like shit.

The Foil

Guy Clinch was a good guy—or a nice one, anyway. He wanted for nothing and lacked everything. He had a tremendous amount of money, excellent health, handsomeness, height, a capriciously original mind; and he was lifeless. He was wide open. Guy possessed, in Hope Clinch, a wife who was intelligent, efficient (the house was a masterpiece), brightly American (and rich); and then there was the indubitable vigour of the child . . . But when he woke up in the morning there was—there was no life. There was only lifelessness.

The happiest time of Guy's fifteen-year marriage had come during Hope's pregnancy, a relatively recent interlude. She had taken her fifty per cent cut in IQ with complete equanimity, and for a while Guy had found himself dealing with an intellectual equal. Suddenly the talk was all of home improvement, of babies' names, nursery conversions, girlish pinks, boyish blues—the tender materialism, all with a point. Never entirely free of builders, the house now thronged with them, shouting, swearing, staggering. Guy and Hope lived to hormone time. The curtain hormone, the carpet hormone. Her nausea passed. She craved mashed potato. Then the nesting hormone: an abrupt passion for patching, for needle and thread. Seeing the size of her, the barrow boys of Portobello Road (and perhaps Keith Talent had been among them) would summon her to their stalls, saying sternly, masterfully, 'Over here, my love. I got the stuff you want.' And Hope would rootle to the base of damp cardboard boxes—rags of velvet, scraps of satin. In the eighth month, when the furniture had begun its dance round the house, and Hope sat with regal fullness in front of the television, darning and patching (and sometimes saying, 'What am I *doing*?'), Guy consulted his senses, scratched his head, and whispered to himself (and he didn't mean the baby), *It's coming . . . It's on its way.*

Oh, how he had longed for a little girl! In the sparse gloom of the private clinic, the most expensive they could find (Hope distrusted any medical care that failed to stretch searchingly into the four figures: she liked the scrolled invoices, with every paper tissue and soldier of toast unsmilingly itemized), Guy did his share of pacing and napping and fretting, while titled specialists looked in from dinner parties or popped by on their way to rounds of golf. A girl, a girl, just an ordinary little girl—Mary, Anna, Jane. 'It's a girl,' he could hear himself saying on the telephone (to whom, he didn't know). 'Five pounds twelve ounces. Yes, a girl. A little under six pounds.' He wanted to be with his wife throughout, but Hope had banned him from labour and delivery wards alike—for reasons, soberly but unanswerably stated, of sexual pride. The baby showed up thirty-six hours later, at four in the morning. He weighed nearly a stone. Guy was allowed a brief visit to Hope's suite. Looking back at it now, he had an image of mother and son mopping themselves down with gloating expressions on their faces, as if recovering from some enjoyably injudicious frolic: a pizza fight, by the look of it. The child was perfect in every way. And he was a monster.

Guy Clinch had everything. In fact he had two of everything. Two cars, two houses, two uniformed nannies, two silk-and-cashmere dinner-jackets, two graphite-cooled tennis-rackets, and so on and so forth. But he had only one child and only one woman. After Marmaduke's birth, things changed. The baby books had prepared him for this; and so had literature, up to a point. But nothing had prepared him or anybody else for Marmaduke. World-famous paediatricians marvelled at his hyperactivity, and knelt like magi to his genius for colic. Every two hours he feasted noisily on his mother's sore breasts; often he would take a brief nap around midnight; the rest of the time he spent screaming. Only parents and torturers and the janitors of holocausts are asked to stand the sound of so much human grief. When things improved, which they did, though only temporarily (for Marmaduke, already softly snarling with asthma, would soon be emblazoned with eczema), Hope still spent much of her time in bed, with or without Marmaduke, but never with Guy. All night he lay dressed for disaster in one of the two visitor's rooms, wondering why his life had suddenly turned into a very interesting and high-toned horror film (one with a Regency setting, perhaps). His habitual mode of locomotion around the house became the tiptoe. When Hope called his name—'Guy?'—and he replied *Yes?* there was never any answer, because his name now meant *Come here.* He appeared, and performed the necessary errand, and disappeared again. Now, with Hope's requests, the first time of asking sounded like the second time of asking, and the second time of asking sounded like the ninth. Less and less often Guy would try to hoist the baby into his arms (under the doubtful gaze of nanny or night-nurse, or some other of Marmaduke's highly paid admirers), saying, rather self-consciously, 'Hello, man-cub.' Marmaduke would pause, reviewing his options; and Guy's bashfully inquiring face would somehow always invite a powerful eye-poke or a jet of vomit, a savage rake of the nails, or at the very least an explosive sneeze. Guy shocked himself by suspecting that Hope kept the infant's nails long the better to repel him. Certainly his face was heavily scored; he sometimes looked like a brave but talentless rapist. He felt supererogatory. The meeting, the rendezvous, it just hadn't happened.

So two of everything, except lips, breasts, the wall of intimacy, enfolding arms, enfolding legs. But that wasn't really it. What had meant to come closer had simply moved further away. Life, therefore, could loom up on him at any moment. He was wide open.

Guy and Hope had been away twice since the birth, on doctor's advice: their doctor's, not Marmaduke's. They left him in the care of five nannies, plus an even more costly platoon of medical commandos. It had been strange, leaving him behind; Guy fully participated in Hope's dread as the cab made its way to Heathrow. Fear was gradually eased by time, and by half-hourly telephone calls. If you listened closely, everything sounded like a baby crying.

First, Venice, in February, the mist, the cold troubled water— and miraculously carless. Guy had never in his life felt closer to the sun; it was like living in a cloud, up in a cloudy sea. But many of the mornings were sombre in mood and sky (dank, failed), and seemed best expressed by the tortured and touristless air of the Jewish Quarter, or by the weak dappling on the underside of a bridge (where the pale flames pinged like static, briefly betrayed by a darker background)—or when you were lost among the Chinese boxes, the congestion of beauties, and you could have likened yourselves to Shakespearean lovers until there came the sound of a wretched sneeze from an office window nearby, then the nose greedily voided into the hanky, and the resumption of the dull ticking of a typewriter or an adding machine.

On the fifth day the sun burst through again inexorably. They were walking arm in arm along the Zattere towards the café where they had taken to having their mid-morning snack. The light was getting to work on the water, with the sun torpedoing in on every pair of human eyes. Guy looked up: to him the sky spoke of Revelation, Venetian-style. He said,

'I've just had a rather delightful thought. You'd have to set it as verse.' He cleared his throat. 'Like this:
> The sun, the sun, the . . . daubing sun:
> The clouds are putti in its hands!'

They walked on. Hope's oval face looked resolute. The juices in her jaw were already addressing the toasted cheese and ham sandwich she would presently enjoy; then the notebook, the little Amex guide, the creamy coffee. 'Dreadful pun, I suppose,' Guy murmured. 'Oh, God.' A press of sightseers confronted them. As they forged through, with Hope taking the lead, their arms were sundered. Guy hurried to catch up.

'The *tourists*,' he said.

'Don't complain. That's idiotic. What do you think *you* are?'

'Yes, but—'

'Yes but nothing.'

Guy faltered. He had turned to face the water and was craning his neck in obscure distress. Hope closed her eyes long-sufferingly, and waited.

'Wait, Hope,' he said. 'Please look. If I move my head, then the sun moves on the water. My eyes have as much say in it as the sun.'

'. . . *Capisco*.'

'But that means—for everyone here the sun is different on the water. No two people are seeing the same thing.'

'I want my sandwich.'

She moved on. Guy lingered, clutching his hands, and saying, 'But then it's hopeless. Don't you think? It's . . . quite hopeless.'

And he whispered the same words at night in the hotel, and went on whispering them, even after their return, lying in sleep's caboose, seconds before Marmaduke woke him with a clout. 'But then it's hopeless. Utterly hopeless.'

In excellent fettle, in the pink or the blue of boyish good health during their absence, Marmaduke sickened dramatically within a few hours of their return. Even-handedly he dabbled with every virus, every hatching, afforded by that early spring. Recovering from mumps, he reacted catastrophically to his final whooping-cough shot. Superflu followed superflu in efficient relay. Doctors now visited him, unasked and unpaid, out of sheer professional curiosity. At this point, and for no clear reason (Sir Oliver asked if he might write a paper about it), Marmaduke's health radically improved. Indeed, he seemed to shed his sickly self as if it were a dead skin or a useless appendage: from the feverish grub of the old Marmaduke sprang a muscle-bound *wunderkind*, clear-eyed, pink-tongued, and (it transpired) infallibly vicious. The change was all very sudden. Guy and Hope went out one day, leaving the usual gastro-enteritic nightmare slobbering on the kitchen floor; they returned after lunch to find Marmaduke strolling round the drawing-room, watched by several speechless nannies. He appeared to have worked it out that he could cause much more trouble, and have much more fun, in a state of peak fitness. His first move was to dispense with that midnight nap. The Clinches hired more help, or they tried. An ailing baby was one thing; a strappingly malevolent toddler was quite another. Up until now, Guy and Hope's relationship, to the child and to each other, had been largely paramedical. After Marmaduke's renaissance, it became, well— you wouldn't say paramilitary. You'd say military. The only people they could get who stayed longer than a day or two were male nurses sacked from lunatic asylums. Around the house, now, there was a kind of SWAT team of burly orderlies, as well as a few scarred nannies and *au pairs*. Dazedly yet without bitterness, Guy calculated that Marmaduke, now in his ninth month, had already cost him a quarter of a million pounds. They went away again.

This time they flew first-class to Madrid, stayed at the Ritz for three nights, and then hired a car and headed south. The car seemed powerful and luxurious enough; it was, without question, resoundingly expensive. (Hope whaled on the insurance. Guy studied the gold-rimmed document: they would airlift you out on almost any pretext.) But as they cruised, as they cruised and glistened one evening through the sparse forests near the southernmost shore of the peninsula, a great upheaval or trauma seemed almost to dismantle the engine at a stroke—the manifold, the big end? In any event the car was clearly history. Around midnight Guy could push it no longer. They saw some lights: not many, and not bright.

The Clinches found accommodation in a rude *venta*. What with the bare coil of the bulb, the lavatorial damp, the flummoxed bed, Hope had burst into tears before the *señora* was out of the room. All night Guy lay beside his drugged wife, listening. At about five, after an interval reminiscent of one of Marmaduke's naps, the weekend roistering in the bar, the counterpoints of jukebox and Impacto machine, exhaustedly gave way to the shrieking gossip of the yard—with a cluck-cluck here and a whoof-whoof there, here a cheep, there a moo, everywhere an oink-oink. Worst or nearest was a moronic bugler of a cock, playing tenor to the neighbours' alto, with his room-rattling reveille. 'Cock-a-doodle-do', Guy decided, was one of the world's great euphemisms. At seven, after an especially unbearable tenor solo (as if the cock were finally heralding the entrance of some imperial super-rooster), Hope jerked upright, swore fluently and foully, applied valium and eye-mask, and bunched herself down again with her face pressed to her knees. Guy smiled weakly. There was a time when he could read love in the shape of his sleeping wife; even in the contours of the blankets he used to be able to read it . . .

He went outside, into the yard. The cock, the grotesque *gaio*, stood in its coop—yes, inches from their pillows—and stared at him with unchallengeable pomp. Guy stared back, shaking his head slowly. Hens were in attendance, quietly and unquestioningly supportive, among all the dust and rubbish. As for the two pigs, they were yahoos even by the standards of the yard. A dark half-grown Alsatian dozed in the hollow of an old oil-drum. Sensing a presence, the dog jerked upright, waking sudden and crumpled, with sand dried into the long trap of the jaw, and moved towards him with compulsive friendliness. It's a girl, he thought: tethered, too. As he went to pet the animal they became entangled, entangled, it seemed, by the very amiability of the dog, by its bouncing, twisting amiability.

In pastel daubings the new prosperity lay to east and west but this place was kept poor by wind. Wind bled and beggared it. Like the cock, the wind just did its wind thing, not caring wherefore. Hot air rises, cool air fills the space: hence, somehow, the tearing and tugging, the frenzied unzippings of this sandpaper shore. In his tennis shorts Guy stepped off the porch and walked past the car (the car avoided his gaze) on to the tattered croisette. A motorbike, an anguished donkey shackled to its cart—nothing else. The sky also was empty, blown clean, an unblinking Africa of blue. Down on the beach the wind went for his calves like emery; Guy gained the harder rump of damp sand and contemplated the wrinkly sea. It opened inhospitably to him. Feeling neither vigour nor its opposite, feeling no closer to life than to death, feeling thirty-five, Guy pressed on, hardly blinking as he crossed the scrotum barrier; and it was the water that seemed to cringe and start back, repelled by this human touch, as he barged his way down the incline, breathed deep, and pitched himself forward in the swimmer's embrace of the sea . . . Twenty minutes later, as he strode back up the beach, the wind threw everything it had at him, and with fierce joy the sand sought his eyes and teeth, the hairless tray of his chest. A hundred yards from the road Guy paused, and imagined surrendering to it (I may be gone some time), dropping to his knees and folding sideways under the icy buckshot of the air.

He queued for coffee in the awakening *venta*. The daughters of the establishment were mopping up; two men boldly conversed across the length of the dark room. Guy stood straight, barefoot, his skin and hair minutely spangled by the sand. An interested woman, had she been monitoring him with half an eye, might have found Guy Clinch well made, classical, above all healthy; but there was something pointless or needless in his good looks; they seemed wasted on him. Guy knew this. Stocky mat-shouldered Antonio, leaning against the pillar by the door, one hand limp on his round belly—and thinking with complacence of his own blood-red loincloth, with the good shoelace-and-tassel effect down there on the crotch—registered Guy not at all, not at all. And the poling daughters had thoughts only for Antonio, careless, drunken, donkey-flogging Antonio and his crimson bullybag . . . Guy drank the excellent coffee, and ate bread moistened with olive oil, out on the banging porch. He then took a tray in to Hope, who ripped off her mask but lay there with her eyes closed.

'Have you achieved anything yet?'

'I've been swimming,' he said. 'It's my birthday.'

'Many happy returns.'

'Young Antonio here is apparently pretty handy with a spanner.'

'Oh yes? The car's dead, Guy.'

Moments earlier, out on the banging porch, a ridiculous thing had happened. Hearing a rhythmical whimpering in the middle distance, Guy had raised his hands to his temples, as if to freeze-frame the thought that was winding through his head (and he wasn't given to them. He wasn't given to pornographic thoughts). The thought was this: Hope splayed and naked, being roughly used by an intent Antonio . . . Guy had then taken his last piece of bread into the yard and offered it to the canned dog. (He also took another incredulous look at the cock, the stupid *gaio.*) The dog was whimpering rhythmically, but showed no appetite. Dirty and gentle-faced, the bitch just wanted to play, to romp, to fraternize, and just kept tripping on her tether. The length of filthy rope—six feet of it—saddened Guy in a way that Spanish cruelty or carelessness had never saddened him before. Down in the yard here, on a wind-frazzled stretch of empty shore, when the only thing that came free and plentiful was space and distance—the dog was given none of it. So poor, and then poor again, doubly, triply, exponentially poor. *I've found it,* thought Guy (though the word wouldn't come, not yet). *It is . . . I've found it and it's . . . It is—*

'Well?'

'Why don't we stay here? For a few days. The sea's nice,' he said, 'once you're in. Until we get the car fixed. It's interesting.'

Hope's impressive bite-radius now loomed over the first section of grilled bread. She paused. 'I don't believe this. You aren't

going *dreamy* on me, are you, Guy? We're out of here. We are
gone.'

And so it became the kind of day where you call airlines and
consulates and car-hire people in a dreary dream of bad connections
and bad Spanish: that evening, on the helipad at Alicante, Hope
treated Guy to his first smile in twenty-four hours. Actually nearly
all of this was achieved (between meals and drinks and swims) from
the control tower of a six-star hotel further down the coast, a place
full of rich and frisky old Germans, all of whom, in their way (Guy
had to admit), potently reminded him of Marmaduke.

Thereafter it was all quite easy: not clear and not pointful,
but not difficult. Guy Clinch looked around his life for a
dimension through which some new force might propagate.
His life, he found, was tailored, upholstered, wall-to-wall; it was
closed. To the subtle and silent modulations of Hope's disgust, he
started to open it—he started to change his life. A hedged bet,
nothing radical. He stopped doing about half the things he had done
before and walked the streets instead.

Fear was his guide. Like all the others on the crescent Guy's
house stood aloof from the road, which was all very well, which was
all very fine and large. But fear had him go where the shops and flats
jostled interestedly over the gauntlet of stalls, like a crowd,
cordoned by slot-game parlours, disastrous beaneries, soup queues,
army hostels, with life set out on barrows—the voodoo and the
hunger, the dreadlocks and dreadnoughts, the Keiths and Kaths of
the Portobello Road. Naturally Guy Clinch had been here before,
in search of a corn-fed chicken or a bag of Nicaraguan coffee. But
now he was searching for the thing itself.

'TV AND DARTS,' said the sign. 'AND PIMBALL'. The first time
Guy entered the Black Cross he was a man pushing through the
green door of his fear . . . He survived. He lived. The place was
ruined and innocuous in its northern light: six or seven black dudes
playing pool over the damp rag of the baize, the monochrome
sickliness of the whites, old pewtery faces, the twittering fruit
machine, the fuming pie-warmer, the lordly absenteeism of the
barman. Guy asked for a drink in the only voice he had. He made
no adjustments: he didn't tousle his hair or scramble his accent; he

carried no tabloid under his arm. He moved to the pinball table: Eye of the Tiger! A feral Irish youth stood inches away whispering *who's the boss who's the boss* into Guy's ear for as long as he seemed to need to do that. Whenever Guy looked up a dreadful veteran of the pub, his face twanging in the canned rock, stared at him bitterly—no forgiveness there, not ever. The incomprehensible accusations of a sweat-soaked black girl were finally silenced by a five-pound note. Guy drank half of his half of lager, and got out. He took so much fear away with him that there had to be less of it each time he returned. But going there at night was another entry.

Keith was the key: Keith Talent, the tutelary knave and joker, with his darts, his moods, his terrible dog and his terrible eyes— Keith, and his pub charisma. Plainly, Keith had to do something about Guy. With his unmistakable pub anti-charisma, Guy was far too anomalous to be let alone; his height, his raincoat, his accent— all this meant that Keith had to ban him, befriend him, beat him up. Keith had to do *something*. So he pouched his darts one day and walked the length of the bar (regulars were wondering when it would happen), leaned over the pinball table with an eyebrow raised and his tongue between his teeth, and bought Guy a drink. The hip pocket, the furled tenners. Keith's house had many mansions. The whole pub shook to utterly silent applause.

Cheers, Keith! After that, Guy belonged. He sailed in there almost with a flourish and summoned the barman by name. After that, he stopped having to buy drinks for the black girls, and stopped having to buy hash and grass from the black boys. (He used to take the stuff home and bury it in the kitchen bin; he didn't drop it in the gutter for fear that a child or a dog might get hold of it, a needless precaution, because the hash wasn't hash and the grass was just grass . . .) Now he could sit in the damp corner of pub warmth, and watch. Really, the thing about life here was its incredible rapidity of change, with people growing up and getting old in the space of a single week. Here time was a tube train with the driver slumped heavy over the lever, flashing through station after station. Guy always thought it was life he was looking for. But it must have been death—or death awareness, *death candour*. I've found it, he thought. It is mean, it is serious, it is beautiful, it is poor, fully earning every complement, every adjective you care to name.

S o when Nicola Six came into the Black Cross and stood at the bar and raised her veil—Guy was ready. He was wide open.

'*Fuck*,' said Keith, as he dropped his third dart.

The thirty-two-gram tungsten Trebler had pierced his big toe. But there was another arrowman or darter in the Black Cross that day; perhaps this smiling *putto* lurked in the artwork of the pinball table, among its pirates and sirens, its sprites and genies. Eye of the Tiger! Guy gripped the flanks of the machine for comfort or support. The ball scuttled into the gutter. Then silence.

She cleared her throat and inquired of Godfrey the barman, who cocked his head doubtfully.

Keith stepped in—or he limped in, anyway, moving down the bar to fill the silence. Guy watched in wonder.

'We don't sell French fags here, darling,' he said. 'No way. Carlyle!'

A black boy eagerly appeared, and panted in triumph, as if his errand were already run. He was given crisp instructions, and a crumpled fiver.

Keith turned, assessingly. Death wasn't new in the Black Cross (death was everyday), but tailored mourning wear, hats, veils? Keith searched his mind, seemed to search his mouth, for something appropriate to say.

'Bereavement, innit,' he said in the end. 'Nobody close I presume?'

'No. Nobody close.'

'Still. God? Get her a brandy. She needs it! What's your name, sweetheart?'

'Nicola Six.'

'Sex!' said Keith.

'S-*i*-x. Actually it's *Six.*'

'Seeks!' said Keith. 'Relax, Nicky. We get all sorts in here. Hey, *cock*. Guy! High society, innit. Come and be introduced.'

Now Guy moved into her force-field. Intensely he confirmed the upward-glancing eyes, the Flemish nose, the dark down above the egregiously sensual upper lip, and all her eloquence of trouble. She too looked as though she might faint at any moment. 'How do you do?' he said ('Oooh!' said Keith), extending a hand towards the black glove. His fingers hoped for the ampères of recognition but all he felt was a slick softness, a moisture that perhaps someone else had readied. Little Carlyle exploded through the pub doors.

'You must let me pay for these,' she said, removing a glove. The hand that now attacked the cellophane was bitten at the five tips.

'All taken care of,' said Keith.

'I suppose,' Guy said, 'I suppose this is by way of being a wake.'

'Family?' said Keith.

'No. Just a woman I used to work for.'

'Does you credit,' said Keith. 'To show respect for the dead. Comes to us all. The Great Leveller innit.'

They talked on. With a violent jerk of self-reproof, Guy bought more drinks. Keith leaned forward murmuring with cupped hands to light Nicola's second cigarette. But this was soon finished or aborted, and Nicola, with a slow nod, was saying,

'Thank you both. You've been very kind. Goodbye.'

Keith and Guy watched her go: the delicate twist of the ankles, the strength and broad candour of the hips, and the telling concavity of the tight black skirt, in the underspace of the buttocks.

'. . . Extraordinary woman,' said Guy.

'Yeah, she'll do,' said Keith, wiping his mouth with the back of his hand (for he was leaving also).

'You're not—'

Keith turned, in sudden warning. His gaze fell to the hand, Guy's hand (their first touch), which lightly gripped his forearm. The hand now slackened and dropped.

'Come on, Keith,' said Guy with a pale laugh. 'She's just been to a funeral. A girl like that,' he added.

Keith looked him up and down with a critical leer: he wasn't going to begin to tell Guy all the things he didn't know. 'So?' he said. 'A girl like what?' Keith straightened his jacket and sniffed manfully. 'She's begging for it,' he said, as if to the street outside. 'She's dreaming of it. Her? She's *praying* for it.'

Keith pushed his way through the green doors. Guy paused for a moment, a pub moment, and then followed him.

That night, in Lansdowne Crescent, at eight-forty-five, with his twelve-hour tryst with Marmaduke now only minutes away, Guy sat on the second sofa in the second drawing-room with a rare second drink and thought: How will I ever know anything in the middle of all this warmth and space, all this super-shelter? I want to feel like the trampolinist when he drops back to earth and to gravity. To touch the earth with heaviness—just to touch it. God expose us, take away our padding and our room.

Keith followed Nicola out of the Black Cross. Guy followed Keith. I wish to Christ I'd followed Guy, but those were early days.

I have fallen into a promising routine. I can complete a chapter in two days, even with all the field-work I have to do. Every third day I do more field-work and write in my notebook. But I am always writing in my notebook. I have always been a writer, of a kind. Keep telling yourself that. Perhaps to counterbalance the looming bulk of Mark Asprey's corpus (take a real look at it when you can bear to), I have laid out my two publications on the leather-topped desk, next to my humming portable. *On the Grapevine*. *Memoirs of a Listener*. By Samson Young. Samson Young. Me. Yes, you. I can embellish. I can take certain liberties. Yet to invent even the bald facts of a life would be quite beyond my powers. Why?

In fact I'm so excited by the first three chapters—it's all I can do not to Fed-Ex them off to Missy Harter at Hornig Ultrason. There are other publishers I could try, but Ms Missy Harter has always been the most persistent and the most encouraging. Maybe I should call her. I need the advance. I need the money. I hope your strength holds.

Keith came over this morning. He wanted to use the VCR. Of course, he has a VCR of his own (he probably has a couple of dozen, stacked away somewhere); but this was a little bit special. 'I got a video,' he explained. 'I got a wife and all.' Then he produced the tape in its plastic wallet. The front cover showed a man's naked torso, its nether regions obscured by a lot of blonde hair. On the back, various glamour girls gawped and slavered. The sticker said £115.95, though no doubt Keith got it cheap.

It was called *When Scandinavian Bodies Go Mouth Crazy.* The title proved to be accurate—even felicitous. I sat with Keith for a while and watched five middle-aged men sitting around a table talking in Danish or Swedish without subtitles. You could make out the odd word. *Radiotherapie. Handikaptoilet.* 'Where's the remote?' Keith asked grimly. He had need of the Fast Forward. We found the remote but its batteries were dead. Keith had to sit through the whole thing (an educational short, I guessed, about hospital administration). I slipped into the study. When I came back the five guys were still talking. The credits came up. Keith looked at the floor and said, '*Bastard.*'

To cheer him up (among other motives), I applied to Keith for darts lessons. His rates are not low.

I too have need of the Fast Forward. But I must let things come at their chosen velocity. I can eke out Chapter Four with Keith's copious sexual confessions, which, at this stage, are the purest gold.

Guy Clinch was no sweat to pull, to cultivate, to *develop.* Already I've been inside his house. I've met his wife. I got a look at the kid. Whew.

It was easy. Again, fatefully easy. Knowing that Keith would be elsewhere (busy cheating: an elderly widow—also good material), I staked out the Black Cross, hoping Guy would show. For the first time I noticed a joke sign behind the bar. It said: NO FUCKING SWEARING. I ordered an orange juice. One of the black guys—he called himself Shakespeare—was smiling at me with roguery or contempt. Shakespeare is, by some distance, the least prosperous of the Black Cross boogies. The bum's overcoat, the plastic shoes, the never-washed dreadlocks. His hair looks like an onion bhaji. 'You trying to cut down, man?' he slowly asked me. Actually I had to make him say it about four times before I understood. His resined face showed no impatience. 'I don't drink,' I told him. Shakespeare was nonplussed. 'Honest,' I said wearily. 'I'm Jewish. We don't, much.' Gradually, as if controlled by a dial, pleasure filled Shakespeare's eyes—which, it seemed to me, were at least as sanguinary and malarial as my own. One of the embarrassments of my condition is that, while it proscribes all activities such as smoking, drinking, taking drugs and having sex—and in fact restricts me to a fibre diet and twelve hours of sleep a night plus naps—I should end up looking like a polluted satyromaniac in acute withdrawal. I look like Caligula after a very heavy year. What with the grape and the slave-girls and everything, and all those fancy punishments and neat tortures I've been doling out . . .

In came Guy, with a flourish of fair hair and long-rider raincoat. I watched him secure a drink and settle over the pinball table with a stack of coins; I contemplated him; I smugly marvelled at his openness, his transparency. Then I sidled up, placed my twenty pence on the glass (this is the etiquette), and gently said, 'Let's play pairs.' I impressed him with my pinball know how and pinball lore: silent five, two-flip, shoulder-check, and so on. We were practically pals anyway, having both bathed in the sun of Keith's acquaintance, of Keith's pub patronage. And, besides, he was completely desperate, as many of us are these days. In a modern city, when you have nothing to do, it's tough to find people to do nothing with. We wandered out together and did the streets for a while, and then (don't you just love the English?) he asked me home for tea.

Once inside his colossal house I saw several further modes of invasion and consolidation. Everywhere I looked there were beach-heads and bridgeheads. His frightening wife Hope I soon had twirling around my pinkie: I may have looked like a piece of shit Guy had brought back from the pub (on the sole of his shoe) but a little media name-dropping and NY networking soon fixed that. I also met Hope's kid sister, Lizzyboo, and checked her out for possible promotion. I even took a good look at the current *au pair*, a ducklike creature with a promisingly vacuous expression, who might be more my speed. As for the cleaning-lady, Auxiliadora, I didn't mess around: I instantly hired her for the apartment . . .

I sort of hate to say it, but the key to the deal was Mark Asprey. The Clinches were frankly electrified when I let slip my connection to the great man. From the way Hope softened, then hardened,

then softened again, I inferred that her excitement was largely
social (Mark Asprey as dream dinner-guest) or indeed sexual (Mark
Asprey as phantom lover). With Guy the interest seemed to be
purely literary. He had recently seen the latest West End hit, *The
Goblet*, which Asprey was even now escorting to Broadway. Dully
asked by me if he'd liked it, Guy said, 'I cried, actually. Actually, I
cried twice.' Then he added wonderingly, 'To be a writer like that.
Just to do what you want to do.' I fought down an urge to mention
my own two books (neither of which found an English publisher.
Run a damage-check on that. Yes, it still hurts. It still exquisitely
burns).

So one dud writer can usually spot another. When we were
alone together in the kitchen Guy asked me what I did and I told
him, stressing my links with various literary magazines and
completely inventing a fiction consultancy with Hornig Ultrason. (I
can invent: I can lie. So why can't I *invent*?) Guy said, 'Really?
That's interesting.' I sent a kind of pressure wave at him; in fact I
was rubbing my thumb and forefinger together beneath the table
when he said, '*I've* written a couple of things, actually.' 'No
kidding.' 'A couple of stories. Expanded travel notes, really.' 'I'd
certainly be happy to take a look at them, Guy.' 'Really? They
aren't any good or anything.' 'Let me be the judge.' 'They're rather
autobiographical, I'm afraid.' 'Oh,' I said. 'Oh that's OK. It's a
start. Don't worry about *that.*

'The other day,' I went on. 'Did Keith follow that girl?'

'Yes he did,' said Guy instantly. Instantly, because Nicola was
already ever-present in his thoughts. And because love travels at
the speed of light.

'What happened?'

'Nothing. He just talked to her.'

I said, 'That's not what Keith told me.'

'What did he say?'

'It doesn't matter what he said. Keith's a liar, Guy.'

Now here's a pleasing symmetry. All three characters have
given me something they've written. Keith's brochure,
Nicola's diaries, Guy's fiction. Things written for different
reasons: self-aggrandizement, self-communion, self-expression.

One offered freely, one abandoned to chance, one coaxingly procured.

Documentary evidence. Is that what I'm writing? A documentary? As for literary talent, as for the imaginative patterning of life, Nicola Six wins, hands down. She whips us all.

Guy was a cinch. But now I must get into all their houses. Keith will be tricky. Probably, and probably rightly, he is ashamed of where he lives. He will have a rule about it—Keith, with his tenacities, his unguessable grooves and ruts, his lout protocols, criminal codes, fierce brand loyalties, and so on. Keith will naturally be tricky.

With Nicola Six, with the murderee, I have a bold idea. It would be a truthful move, and I *must have* the truth. Guy is reasonably trustworthy; I'll just have to allow for his dreamy overvaluations, his selective blindnesses. But Keith is a liar, and I will be obliged to double-check, or even triangulate, everything he tells me. I must have the truth. There just isn't time to settle for anything less than the truth.

I must get inside their houses. I must get inside their heads. I must go deeper. Oh, deeper.

A word about the weather. We have all known days of sun or storm that make us feel what it is to live on a planet. But the recent convulsions have made us feel what it is to live in a solar system, a galaxy. They have made us feel—and the thought is almost too much to bear—what it is to live in a universe.

Particularly the winds. They tear through the city, they tear through the island, as if softening it up for an exponentially greater violence. In the last ten days the winds have killed nineteen people, and thirty-three million trees.

And now, at dusk, outside my window, the trees shake their heads like disco dancers in the strobe light of night-life long ago.

TODD MCEWEN
DRINKING MEN

Auld Licht

Consider a long and famous river; it teems with salmon and story, winds majestic through the most various of Scotland's shires. Where it passes under several bridges and reflects a suggestion of Georgian elegance, sad tales begin.

Stand on the railway bridge until you tire of the cold and noise and the smell of diesel. Walk down the Marketgate, the Nethergate, through a damp little close, on to the wet ankle-twisting stones of the Nevernevergate. Follow along to the Auld Licht and open the vestibule door—

To find Cameron, peripatetic inspector of 1/4 and 1/5 gills (and as such a servant of Her Majesty), gored and bleeding on the horns of his nightly dilemma: lounge or public?

Lounge

The round shoulders of Cameron become rounder as he broods, shifting from one hoof to the other like a ruminant, on concepts of the lounge: young men in skew-fitting professional clothing, suits made from the upholstery of their company cars; cocktails, an absurd pretension of the Auld Licht; giddy secretaries. Talk of sport among the young men becomes slack-jawed, lewd. Talk of mortgages gives way to back-stabbing and vicious mating talk. Video game, jukebox—they would all start screaming.

Cameron rushes to the door of the public and pulls with all his might.

Public

Camaraderie is forced on men. They have little else in life. Forced especially on the desperate, the unimaginative, who must drink the same drink in the same place every day.

How to be alone in the midst of fellowship? One can turn the other stool, try to indicate with the shoulder one wants privacy. One can snap like a little animal. But this breeds suspicion. In the end one is never left alone.

But neither does camaraderie really exist. It is a creation of racists and war-novelists. Rather, there is an erotism about men drinking together.

Come. Come, you must come with us into our happy love cloud. A public bar is the boudoir of a comic-opera seductress: bulbous atomizers, weird musks, pink flounces. You're dragged in, into it. Resistance yields only remorse and confusion.

Mausoleum

The Auld Licht has something of the air of a mausoleum, to which its immemorial granite exterior contributes. You might peer through the immense key-hole of the outer door and see catafalques dimly lit from clerestory windows. It is well known the Auld Licht is neither more nor less clean and happy a place than the typical Victorian family vault.

And there is something wheat-sheaf and classical urn about Cameron's needs of the place. He is one of those who covet bar paraphernalia. At home he amasses beer-mats, bar-towels, ashtrays and match-holders, for his McKa to take into the next world. Cameron's behaviour in the Auld Licht is Egyptian. Mummy-like he stands, hands close to his chest, cigarette and pint his crook and flail.

What to do in a mausoleum, a temple? If you are not the occupant, you perform rituals.

There is a ritual way you order the life you lead at your rented half-metre of bar. In this rectangle of pleasure your cigarettes and your lighter must be neatly arranged, their edges parallel to the bar towel, if you are fortunate enough to be at one. Your glass must be clean and cool. Three cigarettes must pose out of the packet at differing lengths as they do in commercial advertisement.

See, this is your real home, here in the rectangle of pleasure. Here everything serves YOU, and you rejoice you can pay for it. Everything is neatly *arranged* and you can light your pals' cigarettes with florid gestures you learned from American television.

Everything is neat and you can pantomime these small elegances even though your fingernails are dirty and you haven't washed your hair in days.

Ritual second: the out-of-the-blue wheezing-out of *Och Aye* when you are settled with pint and dram and have arranged properly the rectangle of pleasure. Fag lit you stare wonderingly up through the mirk at the stars that haunt the ceilings of all public houses.

Water Temple

In the rear of the mausoleum is located a small water temple. On entering one is struck by the stark almost Japanese beauty of the bare walls, the serious light sedulously provided by the frosted window-glass, by the strong odour of humanity at its most vulnerable. The floor is of two thick marble slabs, an inch above the surrounding trough, awash in ? some mixture of aqueducted and human liquids. In winter a fine mist rises from the floor.

The damp sterile quiet is inspirational, again reminiscent of the Japanese tea-house, though the nectars here are drunk only by the mighty metropolitan drain. If only that hardy piece of pig-iron could tell its story!

Here is the tomb of men's wish to ignore the Devil's clamour from their faucets.

Blackadder

Cameron raises his glass. Not in a festive way. He raises his glass but instead of drinking from it he looks through the 80/- at the enoranged gaggle of buddies. They are all there: Blackadder, McFag, McHaze, McStink, McDram. As usual they are all there. They are there there there, whether Cameron looks at them through his pint or not, whether he looks at them through his dram or not, whether he looks at them or not, they are there. As usual.

The blonde, composed mainly of teat and crimson lipstick, is bursting out of an affair of turnbuckles and rawhide straps. Her qualifications may only be guessed, as the great part of her is covered with little bags of nuts.

Give us a bag of nuts, says Blackadder.

He is in love with this blonde. For several days has been drinking her health, slowly disrobing, seducing her, removing her chaste covering of nuts, savouring her. Blackadder hates nuts but he aches for this woman, for a kiss of her in her contraption.

He was deeply in love with her predecessor, a thong-clad jungle maiden who prowled a tropic pool. Blackadder had munched himself halfway through her downfall when to his disgust an old woman blundered into the Auld Licht and purchased many bags of nuts for a group of children who caterwauled outside. In an instant the all of his Rider Haggard beauty was revealed to Blackadder. He was furious.

You bloody stupid old cow!

Shut your mou, you drunken horror, said the old lady, I've a right to buy nuts.

Och, you've ruined it, ruined it for me, said Blackadder.

Blackadder suffers horribly at stool, from the nuts, but now that the conventional charms of this Sadian beauty are coming clear, his appetite for them grows even stronger. He studies Cameron, sidelong. He feels in his pocket, weighing the budget.

Cameron feels the red eyes of Blackadder upon him. He hunches over his pint and dram, he considers drawing the bar towel up to his chin like a blanket.

Now look at that would you, says Blackadder. Wouldnae ye like tae get yer Muckle Flugga intae her Sma' Glen?

Cameron dares not to move.

Aye ye would, says Blackadder, and yer Gorbals intae her Inner Hebrides, yer Craigenputtock intae her Holy Loch, yer Mons Meg intae her Out Skerries, yer Cairnpapple between her Beattocks. Eh?

Cameron smokes and squints.

Yer Stac Lee in her Burntisland? Have some nuts, says Blackadder, jingling.

No.

On me.

No thank you.

A bag of nuts! Blackadder calls out.

The barman Knox assaults the blonde. Blackadder wrestles with the sealed bag. He has to bite it.

We'll share them, man.

He pushes the bag at Cameron and turns back to the love of his life, a further 9 cm^2 disrobed.

Och now you're talking. Look at her! I wouldnae mind crossin ma Bonar Bridge tae get a look at her Altnaharrie.

McDram giggles chestily from the snooker table where he lies on his face.

Eh! Would you now! says Blackadder, turning round, searching for agreement.

Cameron does not want to move his body, for fear it will further excite Blackadder. He remains in an attitude of willed hibernation.

Knox has never spoken.

Blackadder is the only moving thing in the Auld Licht as he turns a load of nuts and 80/- into a slurry in his maw. The air is cold and stale. Things smoke.

Blackadder's glass is only barely depleted, but he begins to wonder if he has enough money for another, as well as for another bag of nuts, so as to reveal completely the perverse charms of Bambi.

He has so named her.

While Blackadder slithers in the Turkish bath of his desire, Cameron struggles with sorrow. The lumps on the outside of his jacket are not his shoulders, but the signs of inner struggle. Inside him his soul is throwing punches and the dents remain.

Dark is the day. Knox has no need of lantern light. Silence. Outside, wind: the mists of the past.

What you doing in here anyway? says Blackadder.

Cameron's sorrow has made an area of low pressure within him. He feels he must speak, even if it is to Blackadder.

I am about to go on holiday.

Oh? Where are you off to?

No place special.

There's an idea, pint of special! calls Blackadder. And a bag of nuts!

I don't want any, says Cameron.

Nonsense, it's your *hols*, man. And I want to see a bit more of that.

Do you think of nothing but? says Cameron.

Why bother? says Blackadder. It all comes down to that. All. Yer health.

Blackadder insisted his every glass be left empty in front of him. The score: glasses 8, Blackadder 0.

To hell, thinks Cameron. He drinks. He lights up. He wheezes out Och Aye. Blackadder crunches and slurps.

Tobacco

Cameron reflects he is giving up smoking. The way to do it: limit not your cigarettes but your matches. Aye. Matches are the thing. Cameron's McKa knows matches inside out.

Cameron asks for two brands of matches. He takes the one brand out of the one box and puts them in the other, and the reverse. Now he pats them. Blackadder flushes.

What you doin that for? he spits.

The Gander strike better on the Locomotive box, says Cameron, and vice-versa.

Blackadder growls, I've no time for activities of that nature.

He has been sitting in the Auld Licht for three hours and has smoked twenty-five cigarettes. Yet he speaks thus.

I must get back to my pipe, says Cameron.

Again, he ruminates: he is giving up smoking by limiting his matches. Though this morning he stopped to accept a light from the torch of a welder crawling in the sewer. He is smoking more than ever. But he has reduced his match budget to twelve pence per week.

Och well, it's something.

He lives in the 1980s; he worries about his health. The best thing is to destroy it and be done.

GRAHAM SMITH
THE PUB

For the last eight years I have photographed in Middlesbrough, nowhere else. Like my parents I was born and brought up in the town. My father, mother, stepfather and their friends are all good drinkers, and they have always used the same few pubs, which we consider to be the best in Middlesbrough. They are used by those who live on the edge, whose future is the next good time, the next good drink. It's never clear to me why I photograph in these pubs. It might be that I'm using the camera as a way of looking at friends, family, people from their past and, in turn, my background. The truth might be that the camera is just an extension of my drinking arm.

There is no doubt that the camera is an intrusion, and there are always those who are made nervous by it—and some with good reason—but, somehow, I have been tolerated over the years: 'It's just Graham getting off with his camera.' Or: 'It's just the camera man, he's got no film in.' Or: 'Lend us a quid, mate.' And sometimes: 'If he takes one more photo of me I'll tell him!' Anyway I've inherited, worked for and earned my entrance fee, my membership card if you like, and up to now I haven't abused anybody enough to have this card taken away from me.

RAYMOND
CARVER
FRIENDSHIP

Left to right: Tobias Wolff, Raymond Carver and Richard Ford.

Boy, are these guys having fun! They're in London, and they've just finished giving a reading to a packed house at the National Poetry Centre. For some time now critics and reviewers who write for the British papers and magazines have been calling them 'Dirty Realists', but Ford and Wolff and Carver don't take this seriously. They joke about it just as they joke about a lot of other things. They don't feel like part of a group.

It's true they are friends. It's also true they share some of the same concerns in their work. And they know many of the same people and sometimes publish in the same magazines. But they don't see themselves as belonging to, or spearheading, a movement. They are friends and writers having a good time together, counting their blessings. They know luck plays a part in all this, and they know they're lucky. But they're as vain as other writers and think they deserve any good fortune that comes their way—though often as not they're surprised when it happens. Between them they have produced several novels, books of short stories and poems, novellas, essays, articles, screenplays and reviews. But their work, and their personalities, are as different as sea breezes and salt water. It is these differences, along with the similarities, and something else hard to define that make them friends.

The reason they're in London and having such a big time together and not back home where they belong in Syracuse, New York (Wolff), or Coahoma, Mississippi (Ford), or Port Angeles, Washington (Carver), is that they all have books coming out in England within days of each other. Their books are not that much alike—at least I don't feel so—but what the work does have in common, I believe, is that it is uncommonly good and of some importance to the world. And I would go on thinking this even if, God forbid, we should ever cease being friends.

But when I look again at this picture that was taken three years ago in London, after a fiction reading, my heart moves, and I'm nearly fooled into thinking that friendship is a permanent thing. Which it is, up to a point. Now, clearly, the friends in the picture are enjoying themselves and having a good time together. The only serious thing on their minds is that they're wondering when this photographer will finish his business so that they can leave and go about their business of having more fun together. They've made plans for the evening. They don't want this time to end. They're not much looking forward to night and fatigue and the gradual—or sudden—slowing down of things. Truth is, they haven't seen each other for a long time. They're having such a good time being together and being themselves—being friends, in short—they'd like things to just go on like this. To last. And they will. Up to a point, as I said.

That point is Death. Which, in the picture, is the farthest thing from their minds. But it's something that's never that far away from their thinking when they're alone and not together and having fun, as they were that time in London. Things wind down. Things *do* come to an end. People stop living. Chances are that two of the three friends in this picture will have to gaze upon the remains—the *remains*—of the third friend, when that time comes. The thought is grievous, and terrifying. But the only alternative to burying your friends is that they will have to bury you.

I'm brought to ponder such a dreary matter when I think about friendship, which is, in at least one regard anyway, like marriage—another shared dream—something the participants have to believe in and put their faith in, trusting that it *will* go on forever.

As with a spouse, or a lover, so it is with your friends: you remember when and where you met. I was introduced to Richard Ford in the lobby of a Hilton Hotel in Dallas where a dozen or so writers and poets were being housed and fed. A mutual friend—there's a web—the poet Michael Ryan, had invited us to a literary festival at Southern Methodist University. But until the day I got on the plane in San Francisco, I didn't know if I had the nerve to fly to Dallas. After a destructive six-year alcoholic binge, I was venturing out of my hole for the first time since having stopped drinking a few months before. I was sober but shaky.

Ford, however, emanated confidence. There was an elegance about his bearing, his clothes, even his speech—which was poised and courtly and southern. I looked up to him, I think. Maybe I even wished I could be him since he was so clearly everything I was not! Anyway, I'd just read his novel, *A Piece of My Heart,* and loved it and was glad to be able to tell him so. He expressed enthusiasm for my short stories. We wanted to talk more but the evening was breaking up. We had to go. We shook hands again. But the next morning, early, we met in the hotel dining-room and shared a table for breakfast. Richard ordered, I recall, biscuits and country ham along with grits and a side of gravy. He said, 'Yes, ma'am,' or 'No, ma'am,' and 'Thank you, ma'am,' to the waitress. I liked the way he talked. He let me taste his grits. We told each other things, talking through breakfast, coming away feeling we'd known each other, as they say, for a long time.

During the next four or five days we spent as much time together as we could. When we said goodbye on the last day, he invited me to visit him and his wife in Princeton. I figured my chances of ever getting to Princeton were, to put it mildly, slim, but I said I looked forward to it. Still, I knew I'd made a friend, and a good friend. The kind of friend you'd go out of your way for.

Two months later, in January 1978, I found myself in Plainfield, Vermont, on the campus of Goddard College. Toby Wolff, looking every bit as anxious and alarmed as I must have looked, had the cell-like room next to my cell in a condemned barracks building that had formerly been used to house rich kids looking for an alternative to the usual college education. We were there, Toby and I, for a two-week residency and were then expected to go home and work with five or six graduate students through the mail, helping them to write short stories. It was thirty-six degrees below zero, eighteen inches of snow lay on the ground, and Plainfield was the coldest place in the country.

No one, it seems to me, could have been more surprised to find himself at Goddard College in Vermont in January than Toby or I. In Toby's case he was there only because the writer who was supposed to be on board had to cancel at the last minute because of illness. But the writer had suggested Toby in his stead. And not only did Ellen Voight, the director of the programme, invite Toby, sight unseen, but miracle of miracles, she took a chance on a recovering alcoholic still in the early stages of getting well.

The first two nights in the barracks, Toby had insomnia and couldn't sleep. But I liked the way he didn't complain and could even joke about having given up sleep. And I was drawn to him too,

I think, because of what I sensed to be his vulnerability; in certain ways he was even more vulnerable than I was, and that's saying something. We were in the company of writers, fellow faculty members, who were, some of them, among the most distinguished in the country. Toby didn't have a book out, though he had published several stories in the literary magazines. I'd published a book, a couple in fact, but I hadn't written anything in a long time and didn't feel much like a writer. I remember waking up at five one morning, suffering my own anxieties, to find Toby at the kitchen table eating a sandwich and drinking some milk. He looked deranged and as if he hadn't slept in days, which he hadn't. We were glad of each other's uneasy company. I made us some cocoa and we began to talk. It seemed important to be telling each other things there in the kitchen that morning; it was still dark outside and so cold we could hear the trees snap from time to time. From the little window over the sink we could see the northern lights.

For the remaining days of the residency, we hung out when we could, taught a class on Chekhov together and laughed a lot. We both felt we'd been down on our luck, but felt too that our luck just might be changing. Toby said I should come and see him if ever I got to Phoenix, and of course I said sure. Sure. I mentioned to him that I'd met Richard Ford not too long before, who, it turned out, was good friends with Toby's brother, Geoffrey, a man I was to meet and become friends with myself a year or so later. The web again.

In 1980 Richard and Toby became friends. I like it when my friends meet, take a liking to each other and establish their own friendship. I feel all the more enriched. But I can recall Richard's reservation, just before meeting Toby: 'I'm sure he's a good guy,' Richard said. 'But I don't *need* any more friends in my life right now. I have all the friends I can accommodate. I can't do right by my old friends as it is.'

I've had two lives. My first life ended in June 1977, when I stopped drinking. I didn't have many friends left by then, mostly casual acquaintances and drinking pals. I'd lost my friends. Either they'd faded away—and who could blame them?—or else they'd simply plummeted out of sight and, more's the pity, I don't think I even missed them or noted their passing.

Would I choose, saying I had to choose, a life of poverty and ill health, if that was the only way I could keep the friends I have? No. Would I give up my place on the lifeboat, that is to say, die, for any one of my friends? I hesitate, but again the answer is an unheroic no. They wouldn't, any of them, for me either, and I wouldn't have it any other way. We understand each other perfectly in this, and in most other ways as well. Partly we're friends because we *do* understand that. We love each other, but we love ourselves a little more.

Back to the picture. We're feeling good about ourselves and about other things in our life as well. We like being writers. There's nothing else on earth we'd rather be, though we've all been something else too at one time or another. Still, we like it enormously that things have worked out so that we can be together in London. We're having fun, you see. We're friends. And friends are supposed to have a good time when they get together.

What The Doctor Said

He said it doesn't look good
he said it looks bad in fact real bad
he said I counted thirty-two of them on one lung before
I quit counting them
I said I'm glad I wouldn't want to know
about any more being there than that
he said are you a religious man do you kneel down
in forest groves and let yourself ask for help
when you come to a waterfall
mist blowing against your face and arms
do you stop and ask for understanding at those moments
I said not yet but I intend to start today
he said I'm real sorry he said
I wish I had some other kind of news to give you
I said Amen and he said something else
I didn't catch and not knowing what else to do
and not wanting him to have to repeat it
and me to have to fully digest it
I just looked at him
for a minute and he looked back it was then
I jumped up and shook hands with this man who'd just given me
something no one else on earth had ever given me
I may even have thanked him habit being so strong

Raymond Carver

TESS GALLAGHER
RAYMOND CARVER,
1938 TO 1988

Even though I don't choose to express the loss in this way, I understand Leonard Bernstein's having gone to bed and stayed there for six months after his wife died of cancer. But in my family no one would be so indulged. You have to get up, make an effort at normalcy, do your share, and how you feel doesn't come into it . . . part of the working-class ethic, I suppose. But that's where both Ray and I come from. Ray once said to me, speaking about the days before we met, 'I never had *time* to have a nervous breakdown.' The 'iron will' which he says in one of his poems is necessary for making art must, I think, have been forged during just such times when there was 'no-choice-but-to-go-ahead'.

But Ray and I learned somehow to do more than just go ahead; we learned how to go ahead with hope. When we joined lives nearly eleven years ago in El Paso, Texas, we were both recovering from an erosion of trust and hope. Between us I think we'd left behind something like thirty years of failed marriage. We more than rebuilt trust. We got to a place where trust was second nature. But along the way, we had a saying that helped us. We used to say: 'Don't get weird on me, Babe. Don't get weird.' And believe me, by then we'd both lived enough to know what weird was.

You probably know the story. Ray'd been off alcohol about a year when we began to live together. He was shaky. He didn't know if he'd ever write again. He literally ran from the phone when it rang. He'd been bankrupt three times. I can still remember how his eyes lit up when he saw my VISA Card.

I think now we built and rebuilt on Ray's capacity for joy, which extended even to the ability to take immense pleasure in someone else's pleasure, and this capacity continued into his last days. But it hadn't always been this way. Since his death I've become the repository for many people's memories and stories about Ray. I've read in letters from friends he knew during what he called his 'Bad Raymond' days that he was, according to one writer, 'the most unhappy man I'd ever met.' Twenty years later the two met again and the friend was astonished at the transformation.

Theodore Roethke said, 'The right thing happens to the happy man,' and I was privileged to witness as Ray became that happy man. I'm often remembering how glad he was to be alive, and because he was happy to be alive Ray grieved to be leaving his life so early. I won't hide that from you. If will alone could have prevailed, he'd be alive today and with us.

Still, at each turn during his illness he asked: What can I do with the life that's left? He chose to work, to write his poems, in spite of the terror of a brain tumour and later, in June, of the recurrence of cancer in the lungs. His response to that blow was to think of something important to celebrate, and on 17 June we were married in Reno, Nevada. It was a very Carveresque affair, held in the little Heart of Reno Chapel across from the court-house. Afterwards we went gambling at Harrah's Club and with every turn of the wheel I won. I couldn't stop winning.

Near the end Ray knew, he was sure, that his stories were going to last: 'We're out there in history now, Babe,' he said, and he felt lucky to know it. He had a period of clear celebration when his book of stories, *Where I'm Calling From*, came out last spring. There was a brief interlude when we were free from the mental suffering that accompanied his disease and during which he accepted joyously and gratefully the wonderful reviews, induction into the American Academy of Arts & Letters, a Doctorate of Letters from the University of Hartford and the Brandeis Medal for Excellence.

I'm in mourning and celebration for the artist and the man, and also for that special entity which was our particular relationship which allowed such a beautiful alchemy in our lives, a kind of luminous reciprocity. We helped, nurtured and protected each other, and what's more, in the Rilkian sense, we guarded and respected each other's solitude. In our days we were always asking: *What really matters?*

Ray gave me encouragement to write stories and I gave him encouragement to write his stories and his poems, poems through which he out worked his own spiritual equanimity, for he was, I think, at his death, one of those rare, purified beings for whom, as Tolstoy says, the only response is love. He lived every day with the assurance and comfort that I cherished him. As Simone de Beauvoir said, when challenged by feminists for her devotion to Sartre and his work: 'But I *like* to work in the garden next to mine.' I'll miss working in that strange, real garden—Ray's garden. Everything I ever gave there I got back in his gifts of attention to my own work. It has sustained me since his death to be putting his last book in order. I'll miss his delight and laughter in the house and his unfailing kindness, for he was, before anything, my great friend.

All those qualities you sensed about Raymond Carver, that he was a man who would do the decent, the right and generous thing— that was how he was. I can tell you from inside the story. He was like that. And he managed this in a rather complicated life. For his hardships didn't all end back there in the bad old days, and the nature of those hardships is recorded in his stories and poems.

In the last book he completed, one of the epigraphs is a quote from Robert Lowell which reads: 'Yet why not tell it like it happened?' I see this as central to Ray's attitude towards his art and its relation to his life. He carried some burdens of guilt about 'what had happened', and he worked out his redemption and consequently some of ours in his art.

A few days after Ray's death I went into his study in Port Angeles. The study he'd always dreamed of, with a fireplace and a view of valley and mountain, then water beyond. I sat at the desk awhile. Just sat. Then I reached down and pulled open a drawer. Inside I found a dozen folders full of ideas for stories that would have carried him well into the year 2015. I'm sad we won't be reading those stories. But I can't stay in that sadness long. I keep feeling how much, in such a short time, how incredibly much he gave! We have to accept the blessing of that, and Ray believed that he had been graced and blessed and that he had done his utmost to return that blessing to the world. As he has.

I was standing with a friend at Ray's graveside overlooking the Strait of Juan de Fuca a week after his death, and the friend remembered a line from Rilke and said it aloud. It seemed to express the transformation Ray has come to now: 'And he was everywhere, like the evening hour.' To conclude I'd like to present the last poem in his new manuscript.

Late Fragment

And did you get what
you wanted from this life, even so?
I did.
And what did you want?
To call myself beloved, to feel myself
beloved on the earth.

NIK COHN
DELINQUENT IN
DERRY

The winter I turned eleven I came upon a certain snake in the street. This was in Londonderry, Northern Ireland, where I grew up and where no snakes should have been.

Time has blurred the context. Exactly what led me to the snake in question, how I even happened inside its neighbourhood, I can't now imagine. All I remember is that I was walking by myself on an empty backstreet after dark and this street was dim and shuttered, curfew-silent, the way that all good Protestant streets in Derry were meant to be. It must have been a Thursday, the day we ran cross-country at school, because my feet ached. Anyhow. At a given moment I turned a blind corner, and I blundered on the snake.

I didn't register it right away. I was dazzled by bright lights and the enormity of where I was. My feet had brought me to the one place where no soul who hoped to be saved must ever venture—the downtown end of The Strand, hard by the docks, on the borders of the Bogside, the Papist war zone.

I had no idea what made it a plague-spot. But a plague-spot it was. Tiggle, the janitor, said as much. So did McAlee, the man who did the drains. In the walled fastness of Magee, the college where my father taught French, it was freely referred to as an MKS, for Mobile Knocking Shop. And here I was, smack dab at the heart of it. After dark. By daylight, on the few furtive occasions I'd glimpsed it, it had only looked shabby, terminally depressed. But by night it had been transfigured: a style of place I hadn't dared to dream existed.

Directly across the street was a perfect neon inferno, brightly lit and self-contained like a stage-set: Rock 'n' Roll blasting from the open doors of coffee bars; beehive blondes with sky-blue or scarlet skirts and bright orange lipstick; sailors hunting in packs; leather boys, motorbikes, the reek of diesel.

Nothing had prepared me, not remotely. Derry, before the Provos and long before Bloody Sunday, was a backwater some thirty to fifty years behind the moment and proud of it. As for Magee itself, its isolation was almost monastic. Nobody owned a television, precious few a gramophone; and, although my father read the *Irish Times* each morning in the college library, my own hot news came entirely from the *Dandy* and the *Eagle*: Dan Dare had landed on Mars, Wyatt Earp was Sheriff in Tombstone and

Desperate Dan had made himself ill by devouring a box of six-inch nails, believing them to be sweet cigarettes. Once, when I was four, I'd caught a whiff of *Put Another Nickel In*, Teresa Brewer, courtesy of a passing bus, and my mother had had to drag me off the street by force. But at the moment I had stumbled on to The Strand, in 1957, the only pop singer I'd heard of was Rita Murray, and then only because she came from Belfast.

So I froze. If I'd been transported here by a time machine, I could not have been more out of place. Immediately I understood that my role was as a voyeur, a worshipper at one remove, and I snuck back inside an unlit doorway, from which, in safety, I could watch unobserved—see and not be seen.

Only then did I notice the snake. From deep inside the chasm of the Roseland Café a jukebox let loose with *Tutti Frutti*, Little Richard, and on the pavement outside an impromptu jitterbug broke out. Teenagers in fancy dress, whom I later learned were Teddy Boys, began to jive with each other, males with males, in a craze of flashing fluorescent socks and shocking-pink drapes, drain-pipes and blue suede shoes; and as they whirled they kept passing the snake, which I took at first to be a whip or a length of elastic tubing, back and forth like a baton.

When the music died out, so did the dancing. But the snake remained, dangled beneath a street lamp, framed and backlit by the Roseland's plate-glass window. I could now see it clearly. It appeared to be about two feet long, with a tapering greenish coil for a body and a great, black hooded skull. Something between a cobra and a python, I guessed, and it twirled and corkscrewed, stretched and contracted in rhythm, twined around a blue mohair sleeve with a purple velvet cuff.

It didn't seem a discovery, exactly. Recognition was more like it. It was as if there was something I had always known, only I'd forgotten or misplaced it, let it escape me; and now the snake, and everything that went with the snake, had restored it.

The something in question had no name, of course. And I did not try to give it one. All I thought consciously was that I now possessed a secret, and this secret made me powerful, in some way superior.

The feeling was not familiar. In my pre-Strand existence, secret power was the last thing I thought to possess. On the contrary, I was consumed by not belonging, by having no place, either in Derry or anywhere else on Planet Earth. In this, I had support: 'Unfit to fit', some kindergarten *confrère* once carved into the lid of my desk, and the motion seemed to be carried by acclamation.

Part of the problem was genetic. By birth and upbringing I was an Anglo-Teutonic Russian Menshevik Agnostic Jew, and pretty much typical of the type. Born in London, weaned in Scotland and South Africa, I didn't arrive in Ireland until I was five, and somehow I never fully acclimatized. Certainly not in native eyes, at any rate. My father wrote books about heretics, my mother had an accent, and I myself was neither Protestant nor Catholic, not Irish but also nothing else. In the context of Derry and, in particular, of Foyle, the moth-eaten Presbyterian shrine in decline where I went to school, I might as well have come from Mars—the man who fell to Earth and, abysmally, failed to bounce.

Magee completed the curse. In theory it was a training school for Calvinist ministers; in reality, with its high stone walls and imported tutors, more like an unarmed encampment; and its isolation from the town was absolute. Dimly one was conscious of the hatred outside, with its perpetual roundelay of Catholic ambuscades and Protestant reprisals, Black masses and Orange parades. But it seemed to carry no reality. If it had not been for Tiggle, the janitor, my only link to life beyond Magee's walls, I would hardly have been aware that men, when shot, did actually bleed.

Always, the key was that I myself took no part. From my very earliest remembrance—in which my twenty-month self enticed a five-year-old gardener's daughter into climbing up a tree and getting stuck, thus allowing me to study from below the effects of light and shade on her sky-blue knickers, her sweating spun-gold legs all covered with scabs, ripe and pickable as currants baked into damp bread, also the way in which her screams caused her thighs to shimmy and shudder like blancmange in a gale—my intuition was that my best role was not to perform but always to

173

watch, preferably from a distance.

There was one exception. At Magee, down by Tiggle's cottage and the tennis court where he died, there was an outhouse with a long and flat cement exterior wall, and up against this wall, every rainless afternoon after school, I used to bat a tennis ball. Sometimes I would hit it with a rot-gutted racket as flaccid as a butterfly net, sometimes with a sawn-off broomstick or the flat of a cricket bat, and sometimes, when times were tough, with a cabbage-stalk soaked in brine; and as I hit, I counted.

The formula never varied. First I would attempt to execute one hundred strokes on my forehand, then another hundred backhand, then forehand again, then backhand, and so interminably on, until at last I missed, at which point I'd go back to the beginning, starting over from stroke one.

What was the use? I'm still not sure. No special target was involved, no astronomical figure whose attainment would somehow release me. There was no question of athletic prowess. On the contrary, in my passion not to flub, I kept all my shots as passive and pattycake as possible, never dared the slightest variation. Avoiding error was not the main thing, it was the only thing, and so metronomic was the thud of ball on wall, I might have been marking time.

Faced with such futility, even the mildest divinity students were goaded beyond endurance. With time I acquired a regular gallery of hecklers, beseeching me, just once, to give the ball a free and hearty whack. But I never did. The very soullessness of this unending putt-puttery was its perverse pleasure. One afternoon, halfway through my 700th on the forehand, Tiggle keeled over in mid-imprecation, belly-up and purple-headed, with a pale pink froth about his lips that was like the lees of lemonade sherbet. There were murmurings of manslaughter, and these I took as a compliment.

For years the ceremony never varied. Then I came out into The Strand, observed the snake, and later, safe back in the sanctuary of Magee, I went down to the outhouse wall. Even though it was now pitch dark, I grabbed a trusty coal shovel, whirled it like a shillelagh. And I began to smash the balls at random. I hit out blindly, possessed. Exploding all about me like so many hand-grenades, balls ricocheted into my face and eyes, my belly; knocked me backwards, drove me to my knees. Ball the wall, indeed I did and the tarmac beneath me, and the air, and all of the darkness, too. I didn't quit till every last ball I owned had been splatted or forever lost. Then I hurled the shovel as high and as far as my mean strength could launch it, and I never played that game again.

I took to travelling, instead. Of a sudden Magee no longer seemed a refuge, only a confinement, and I invented numberless excuses to be free of it, go out scavenging. My feet, for instance. Claiming incipient droopage of the instep, I won permission to pay a weekly visit after Friday school to one Bernard Dinty, a cobbler turned foot-healer.

Dinty's office, a bare white room above a flesher's on Shipquay Street, lay deep within the walled city, overlooking the Bogside, and it hid behind drawn blinds. There I would be marched back and forth across a narrow strip of linoleum, one full hour by the clock, practising posture, balance and what Dinty termed tone of gait.

This office, it was rumoured, doubled as a front for a butter-smuggling ring. And it was true there was something rancid and furtive in its air, a smell of dirty little secrets. As for the healer himself, a rumpled little squit of a man, all polka dot bow-tie and stained white medico's coat, he liked to soundtrack my perambulations with lectures on the evils of masturbation and of patronizing brothels or, as he preferred, the Temples of Venus. 'Fallen arches today, fallen women next Saturday,' was his motto, and, each time he delivered it, he would touch my bare short-trousered leg above the knee, not so much sweating as oozing, clammily steaming, like an overheated jam pudding in melt-down.

My compensation was that, by the time I won release, it would be after dark, all the streets would have changed for night, and the straightest, safest way home would lead me directly past the Roseland Café.

The snake itself, I never saw again. But the Teddy Boys, its votaries, were regulars, and they came to embody everything I sensed, everything that I still couldn't spell.

In their daytime incarnations, I understood, the Teds were only Papist scum, the delinquent flotsam and jetsam of the Bogside. As such, their life prospects were nil. Foredoomed, dispossessed, they had traded away the Free for the Welfare State, and now they had no work, no home, no hope whatever, unless the fleeting glory of an IRA martyrdom. They were, in every common sense, non-persons. And yet, here on The Strand, in the neon night by Rock 'n' Roll, they were made heroic. In every flash of fluorescent sock or velvet cuff, every jive-step swagger for Chuck Berry, every leer and flaunt of their greased pompadoured ducktails, they beggared the fates, made reality irrelevant.

My enthusiasm was unshared. At Magee and Foyle, such stuff was viewed as indecency and shame. And this, of course, became its clinching attraction. Like everything else that I was equipped to love, the Roseland must be kept my own secret.

The second step was Elvis.

Again, I had Bernard Dinty partly to thank. Late one Friday dusk, heading for my weekly treadmill, I let myself loiter outside the fly-blown windows of McCafferty's, Journals & Uncommonly Fine Books, Ltd, and there sat a copy of *Titbits*, a weekly yellow tabloid barred by my mother as 'cheap and nasty', therefore a jewel beyond price. On its cover was a head-and-shoulders glossy of the King.

In the first shock of impact I was conscious only of the mouth, in particular the upper lip. This seemed to loom disembodied, in the style of a Cheshire cat grin, only twisted and lopsided, as serpentine as any real or rubber snake, so that its smile became a sneer. And this sneer said: 'Oh, yeah?'

To which echo answered: 'Oh, yeah!' It seemed to me then, it seems to me still, the wisest remark ever made. In that instant, I accepted Elvis Presley to be my personal living saviour and nothing has happened since to change my mind, or bruise my faith.

What I saw in him, beyond sheer physical gorgeousness, was the possibility of the impossible. The upper lip, the sneer were a direct extension of the Teddy Boys and Roseland. For Elvis, I sensed at once and soon discovered for a fact, was derived from the same unregarded stable. He too had started out foredoomed, dispossessed, the most hopeless of White Trash. His ambition had been to grow up into a truck driver. Specifically, he'd lusted after the peaked mesh caps that truckers affected; he'd thought these made them look daring. Also, he'd envied their freedom. But such heroics, he understood, were beyond him. In the crunch, he was too soft-skinned, too scared, too much a mother's boy. A true trucker he could never be. So he became a Messiah instead.

Now my pilgrimage began in earnest. But it did not prove easy going. For Protestant Derry, home of the Apprentice Boys, Rock 'n' Roll was poison. The Teddy Boy riots over *Blackboard Jungle* and Bill Haley in England had panicked all of loyalist Ulster. This was not just a teenage rebellion that loomed: it was as if the massed forces of Satan had been unleashed, threatening to wipe out all sanity, all sanctity—in the words of *The Derry Sentinel,* all 'Civilization as we know it.'

All Rock shows, artifacts and films were outlawed. And anyone who challenged this suppression was in for a bumpy ride. Mary Fadden, a comely fifth-former at Northlands, the local girls' school, was expelled for secreting a picture of Jerry Lee Lewis in her desk; discs and posters fuelled bonfires; and Elvis himself was ceremonially torched in effigy at the Brandywell Football Grounds, nailed to a flaming cross. Only Catholics, since idolatry was their nature, were free to devil-worship in peace.

What to do? There seemed only one solution. So my feet took a turn for the worse. In reality, I had ceased to frequent Dinty after a session at which, suggesting that I might benefit from being fitted with metal instep supports, he insisted on taking my inner-thigh measurements. For public consumption, however, I now increased my visits from weekly to almost nightly and, with the freedom thus gained, I went exploring.

Across the river, in a Catholic enclave in the Waterside district, there was a disused funeral home in which, three nights a week, at 6d a shot, contraband Teen movies could be sat through and sometimes seen, according to the state of the projector. One drawback was that a cross-pollination of embalming fluid and scented wax flowers still hung in the air, an intimation of mortality sickly-sweet enough to turn the most fanatic stomach. Still, hunched in the suffocating dark, I drowned myself in *Don't Knock The Rock, The Girl Can't Help It* and *I Was A Teenage Werewolf,* had a crush on Eddie Cochran but chose to marry Sheree North.

The Crypt, as it was aptly named, was just the start. By perching myself atop a step-ladder, then balancing the family steam-wireless on a stack of Encylopaediae Britannicae, 1911, in thirty-four volumes, I could jam my left ear tight up against the sound-box, four inches below my bedroom ceiling, and so receive the faintest static-riddled crackling of Radio Luxemburg, a thousand miles away across Europe; at Thos. Mullen, Tonsorial Artist, on Ferryquay Street, back copies of *Titbits* and *Men Only* tutored me in the hit parades, also in anatomy ('Petunia, 19, is an artist's model and this is one pulchritudinous petal that any Old Master would be proud to pluck'); and at last one night at the Palace, the first cinema in town openly to dare show an Elvis film, halfway through the *Teddy Bear* sequence in *Loving You*, I heard a siren shrieking above, looked up from my lair in the back stalls and saw the balcony overhead shaking, literally buckling, from sheer humping tonnage of wet-knickered nymphs. 'Earthquake!' the inevitable alarmist hollered and a minor stampede ensued, cravens of all persuasions scrabbling wholesale for the exits, like so many extras from *The Last Days of Pompeii*.

I myself failed to budge. For this, I knew well, was no earthquake or even holocaust—it was the end of the world. Or leastways, of civilization as we knew it.

ANGELA CARTER
'TIS PITY SHE'S A
WHORE

There was a rancher who had two children, a son and then a daughter. A while after that, his wife died and was buried under two sticks nailed together to make a cross because there was no time, yet, to carve a stone.

Did she die of the loneliness of the prairies? Or was it anguish that killed her, anguish, and nostalgia for the close, warm, neighbourly life she had left behind her when she came to this emptiness? Neither. She died of the pressure of that vast sky, that weighed down upon her and crushed her lungs until she could not breathe any more, as if the prairies were the bedrock of an ocean in which she drowned.

She told her boy: 'Look after your sister.' He, blond, solemn, little; he and Death sat with her in the room of logs her husband split to build. Death, with high cheek-bones, wore his hair in braids. His invisible presence in the cabin mocked the existence of the cabin. The round-eyed boy clutched his mother's dry hand. The girl was younger.

Then the mother lay with the prairies and all that careless sky upon her breast, and the children lived in their father's house. So they grew up. In his spare time, the rancher chiselled at a rock: 'Beloved wife of . . . mother of . . .' beneath the space at the top he had left for his own name.

America begins and ends in the cold and solitude. Up here, she pillows her head upon the Arctic snow. Down there, she dips her feet in the chilly waters of the South Atlantic, home of the perpetually restless albatross. America, with her torso of a woman at the time of this story, a woman with an hour-glass waist, a waist laced so tightly it snapped in two, and we put a belt of

---

Note: John Ford: 1586–circa 1639. English dramatist of the Jacobean period. His tragedy, *'Tis Pity She's a Whore*, was published in 1633. 'Deep in a dump John Ford alone was got/With folded arms and melancholy hat.' (*Choice Drollery*, 1656.)

John Ford: 1895–1973. American film-maker. Filmography includes: *Stagecoach* (1939); *My Darling Clementine* (1946); *She Wore a Yellow Ribbon* (1949). 'My name is John Ford. I make Westerns.' (*John Ford*, Andrew Sinclair, New York 1979.)

water there. America, with your child-bearing hips and your crotch of jungle, your swelling bosom of a nursing mother and your cold head, your cold head.

Its central paradox resides in this: that the top half doesn't know what the bottom half is doing. When I say the two children of the prairie, suckled on those green breasts, were the pure children of the continent, you know at once that they were *norteamericanos*, or I would not speak of them in the English language, which was their language, the language that silences the babble of this continent's multitude of tongues.

Blond children with broad, freckled faces, the boy in dungarees and the little girl in gingham and sun-bonnet. In the old play, one John Ford called them Giovanni and Annabella; the other John Ford, in the movie, might call them Johnny and Annie-Belle.

Annie-Belle will bake bread, tramp the linen clean and cook the beans and bacon; this lily of the West had not spare time enough to pause and consider the lilies of the field, who never do a hand's turn. No, sir. A woman's work is never done and she became a woman early.

The gaunt paterfamilias would drive them into town to church on Sundays with the black Bible on his knee wherein their names and dates of birth were inscribed. In the buggy, his shy, big-boned, tow-headed son in best, dark, Sunday clothes, and Annie-Belle, at thirteen, fourteen, increasingly astonished at and rendered shy by her own lonely flowering. Fifteen. How pretty she was growing! They came to pray in God's house that, like their own, was built of split logs. Annie-Belle kept her eyes down; she was a good girl. They were good children. The widower drank, sometimes, but not much. They grew up in silence, in the enormous silence of the empty land, the silence that swallowed up the Saturday-night fiddler's tune, mocked the rare laughter at weddings and christenings, echoed, a vast margin, around the sermons of the preacher.

Silence and space and an unimaginable freedom which they dare not imagine.

Since his wife died, the rancher spoke rarely. They lived far out of town. He had no time for barn-raisings and church suppers. If she had lived, everything would have been different, but he occupied his spare moments in chiselling her gravestone. They did not celebrate Thanksgiving for he had nothing for which to give thanks. It was a hard life.

The Minister's wife made sure Annie-Belle knew a thing or two when she judged it about the time the girl's bleeding started. The Minister's wife, in a vague, pastoral way, thought about a husband for Annie-Belle, a wife for Johnny. 'Out there, in that little house on the prairie, so lonesome . . . Nobody for those young folks to talk to 'cept cows, cows, cows.'

What did the girl think? In summer, of the heat, and how to keep flies out of the butter; in winter, of the cold. I do not know what else she thought. Perhaps, as young girls do, she thought that a stranger would come to town and take her away to the city and so on, but, since her imagination began and ended with her experience, the farm, work, the seasons, I think she did not think so far, as if she knew already she was the object of her own desire for, in the bright light of the New World, nothing is obscure. But when they were children, all they knew was they loved each other just as surely a brother or a sister should.

She washed her hair in a tub. She washed her long, yellow hair. She was fifteen. It was spring. She washed her hair. It was the first time that year. She sat on the porch to dry her hair, she sat in the rocking-chair which her mother selected from the Sears' Roebuck catalogue, where her father would never sit, now. She propped a bit of mirror on the porch railing. It caught the sun and flashed. She combed out her wet hair in the mirror. There seemed to be an awful lot of it, tangling up the comb. She wore only her petticoat, the men were off with the cattle, nobody to see her pale shoulders except that Johnny came back. The horse threw him, he knocked his head against a stone. Giddy, he came back to the house, leading his pony, and she was busy untangling her hair and did not see him, nor have a chance to cover herself.

'Why, Johnny, I declare—'

Imagine an orchestra behind them: the frame-house, the porch, the rocking-chair endlessly rocking, like a cradle, the white petticoat with eyelet lace, her water-darkened hair hanging on her shoulders and little trickles running down between her shallow breasts, the young man leading the limping pony, and, inexhaustible as light, around them the tender land.

The 'Love Theme' swells and rises. She jumps up to tend him. The jogged mirror falls.

'Seven years' bad luck—'

In the fragments of the mirror, they kneel to see their round, blond, innocent faces that, superimposed upon one another, would fit at every feature, their faces, all at once the same face, the face that never existed until now, the pure face of America.

> EXTERIOR. PRAIRIE. DAY.
> LONG SHOT: Farmhouse.
> CLOSE UP: Petticoat falling on to porch of farmhouse.

Wisconsin, Ohio, Iowa, Missouri, Kansas, Minnesota, Nebraska, the Dakotas, Wyoming, Montana . . . Oh, those enormous territories! That green vastness, in which anything is possible.

> EXTERIOR. PRAIRIE. DAY.
> CLOSE UP: Johnny and Annie-Belle kiss.
> 'Love Theme' up.
> Dissolve.

No. It wasn't like that! Not in the least like that.

He put out his hand and touched her wet hair. He was giddy.

ANNABELLA: Methinks you are not well.

GIOVANNI: Here's none but you and I. I think you love me, sister.

ANNABELLA: Yes, you know I do.

And they thought, then, that they should kill themselves, together now, before they did it; they remembered tumbling together in infancy, how their mother laughed to see their kisses, their embraces, when they were too young to know they should not do it, yet even in their loneliness on the enormous plain they knew they must not do it . . . do what? How did they know what to do? From watching the cows with the bull, the bitch with the dog, the hen with the cock. They were country children. Turning from the mirror, each saw the other's face as if it were their own.

Music plays.
GIOVANNI: Let not this music be a dream, ye gods.
  For pity's sake, I beg you!
  [She kneels.]

ANNABELLA: On my knees,
  Brother, even by our mother's dust, I charge you
  Do not betray me to your mirth or hate.
  Love me, or kill me, brother.
  [He kneels.]

GIOVANNI: On my knees,
  Sister, even by our mother's dust, I charge you
  Do not betray me to your mirth or hate.
  Love me, or kill me, sister.

> EXTERIOR. FARMHOUSE PORCH. DAY.
> Upset water-tub, spilling over discarded petticoat.
> Empty rocking-chair, rocking, rocking.

It is the boy—or young man, rather—who is the most mysterious to me. The eagerness with which he embraces his fate. I imagine him mute or well-nigh mute; he is the silent type, his voice creaks with disuse. He turns the soil, he breaks the wills of the beautiful horses, he milks the cows, he works the land, he toils and sweats. His work consists of the vague, undistinguished 'work' of such folks in the movies. No cowboy, he, roaming the plains. Where the father took root, so has the son, in the soil that was never before broken until now.

And I imagine him with an intelligence nourished only by the black book of the father, and hence cruelly circumscribed, yet dense with allusion, seeing himself as a kind of Adam and she his unavoidable and irreplaceable Eve, the unique companion of the wilderness, although by their toil he knows they do not live in Eden and of the precise nature of the forbidden thing he remains in doubt.

For surely it cannot be this? This bliss? Who could forbid such bliss!

Was it bliss for her too? Or was there more of love than pleasure in it? 'Look after your sister.' But it was she who looked after him as soon as she knew how and pleasured him in the same spirit as she fed him.

GIOVANNI: I am lost forever.

Lost in the green wastes, where the pioneers were lost. Death with his high cheek-bones and his braided hair helped Annie-Belle take off her clothes. She closed her eyes so that she could not see her own nakedness. Death showed her how to touch him and him her. There is more to it than farmyard ways.

> INTERIOR. MINISTER'S HOUSE. DAY.
> Dinner-table. Minister's wife dishing portions from a pot for her husband and her son.
>
> MINISTER'S WIFE: T'ain't right, just ain't right, those two out there, growing up like savages, never seeing nobody.
>
> MINISTER'S SON: She's terribly pretty, Mama.
>
> The Minister's wife and the Minister turn to look at the young man. He blushes slowly but comprehensively.

The rancher knew nothing. He worked. He kept the iron core of grief within him rustless. He looked forward to his solitary, once-monthly drunk, alone on the porch, and on those nights they took a chance and slept together in the log cabin under the patchwork quilt made in the 'log cabin' pattern by their mother. Each time they lay down there together, as if she obeyed a voice that came out of the quilt telling her to put the light out, she would extinguish the candle-flame between her fingertips. All around them, the tactility of the dark.

She pondered the irreversibility of defloration. According to what the Minister's wife said, she had lost everything and was a lost girl. And yet this change did not seem to have changed her. She turned to the only one she loved, and the desolating space around them diminished to that of the soft grave their bodies dented in the long grass by the creek. When winter came, they made quick, dangerous love among the lowing beasts in the barn. The snow melted and all was green enough to blind you and there was a vinegarish smell from the rising of the sharp juices of spring. The birds came back.

A dusk bird went chink-chink-chink like a single blow on the stone xylophone of the Chinese classical orchestra.

> EXTERIOR. FARMHOUSE PORCH. DAY.
> Annie-Belle, in apron, comes out on homestead porch; strikes metal triangle.

> ANNIE-BELLE: Dinner's ready!

> INTERIOR. FARMHOUSE. NIGHT.
> Supper-table. Annie-Belle serves beans. None for herself.

> JOHNNY: Annie-Belle, you're not eating anything tonight. ¦

> ANNIE-BELLE: Can't rightly fancy anything tonight.

The dusk bird went chink-chink-chink with the sound of a chisel on a gravestone.

He wanted to run away with her, west, further west, to Utah, to California where they could live as man and wife, but she said: What about father? He's lost enough already. When she said that, she put on, not his face, but that of their mother, and he knew in his bones the child inside her would part them.

The Minister's son, in his Sunday coat, came courting Annie-Belle. He is the second lead, you know in advance, from his tentative manner and mild eyes; he cannot long survive in this prairie scenario. He came courting Annie-Belle, although his mother wanted him to go to college. What will you do at college with a young wife? said his mother. But he put away his books; he took the buggy to go out and visit her. She was hanging washing out on the line.

Sound of the wind buffeting the sheets, the very sound of loneliness.

> SORANZO: Have you not the will to love?

> ANNABELLA: Not you.

SORANZO: Who, then?

ANNABELLA: That's as the fates infer.

She lowered her head and drew her foot back and forth in the dust. Her breasts hurt, she felt queasy.

> EXTERIOR. PRAIRIE. DAY
> Johnny and Annie-Belle walking on the prairie.

ANNIE-BELLE: I think he likes me, Johnny.

> Pan blue sky, with clouds. Johnny and Annie-Belle, dwarfed by the landscape, hand in hand, heads bowed. Their hands slowly part.

> Now they walk with gradually increasing distance between them.

The light, the unexhausted light of North America that, filtered through celluloid, will become the light by which we see America looking at itself.

Correction: will become the light by which we see *North America* looking at itself.

> EXTERIOR. FARMHOUSE PORCH. DAY.
> Row of bottles on a fence.
> Bang, bang, bang. Johnny shoots the bottles one by one.
> Annie-Belle on porch, washing dishes in a tub.
> Tears run down her face.

> EXTERIOR. FARMHOUSE PORCH. DAY.
> Father on porch, feet up on railing, glass and bottle to hand.
> Sun going down over prairie.
> Bang, bang, bang.

> FATHER'S POINT OF VIEW: Johnny shooting bottles off the fence.

> Clink of father's bottle against glass.

EXTERIOR. FARMHOUSE. DAY.

Minister's son rides along track in long shot. Bang, bang, bang.

Annie-Belle, clean dress, tidy hair, red eyes, comes out of house on to porch. Clink of father's bottle against glass.

EXTERIOR. FARMHOUSE. DAY.

Minister's son tethers horse. He has brushed his Sunday coat. In his hand, a posy of flowers—cottage roses, sweet-brier, daisies. Annie-Belle, smiles, takes posy.

ANNIE-BELLE: Oh! [*Holds up pricked forefinger; blood drops on to a daisy.*]

MINISTER'S SON: Let me . . . [*Takes her hand. Kisses the little wound.*] . . . make it better.

Bang. Bang. Bang.
Clink of bottle on glass.

CLOSE-UP: Annie-Belle, smiling, breathing in the scent from her posy.

And, perhaps, had it been possible, she would have learned to love the Minister's gentle son before she married him, but, not only was it impossible, she also carried within her the child that meant she must be married quickly.

INTERIOR. CHURCH. DAY.

Harmonium. Father and Johnny by the altar. Johnny white, strained; father stoical. Minister's wife thin-lipped, furious. Minister's son and Annie-Belle, in simple white cotton wedding-dress, join hands.

MINISTER: Do you take this woman . . .

CLOSE-UP: Minister's son's hand slipping wedding-ring on to Annie-Belle's finger.

INTERIOR. BARN. NIGHT.
Fiddle and banjo old-time music.
Vigorous square dance going on; bride and groom
lead.

Father at table, glass in hand.
Johnny, beside him, reaching for bottle.

Bride and groom come together at end of dance;
groom kisses bride's cheek. She laughs.

CLOSE-UP: Annie-Belle looking shyly up at the
Minister's son.
The dance parts them again; as Annie-Belle is handed
down the row of men, she staggers and faints.

Consternation.

Minister's son and Johnny both run towards her.

Johnny lifts her up in his arms, her head on his
shoulder. Eyes opening. Minister's son reaches out
for her. Johnny lets him take hold of her.

She gazes after Johnny beseechingly as he disappears
among the crowd.

Silence swallowed up the music of the fiddle and the banjo;
Death with his hair in braids spread out the sheets on the marriage
bed.

INTERIOR. MINISTER'S HOUSE. BEDROOM. NIGHT.
Annie-Belle in bed, in a white night-gown, clutching
the pillow, weeping. Minister's son, bare back, sitting
on side of bed with his back to camera, head in hands.

In the morning, her new mother-in-law heard her vomiting into
the chamber-pot and, in spite of her son's protests, stripped
Annie-Belle and subjected her to a midwife's inspection. She
judged her three months gone, or more. She dragged the girl round
the room by the hair, slapped her, punched her, kicked her, but
Annie-Belle would not tell the father's name, only promised, swore

on the grave of her dead mother, that she would be a good girl in future. The young bridegroom was too bewildered by this turn of events to have an opinion about it; only, to his vague surprise, he knew he still loved the girl although she carried another man's child.

'Bitch! Whore!' said the Minister's wife and struck Annie-Belle a blow across the mouth that started her nose bleeding.

'Now, stop that, mother,' said the gentle son. 'Can't you see she ain't well?'

The terrible day drew to its end. The mother-in-law would have thrown Annie-Belle out on the street, but the boy pleaded for her, and the Minister, praying for guidance, found himself opening the Bible at the parable of the woman taken in adultery and meditated well upon it. Only tell me the name of the father, her young husband said to Annie-Belle.

'Better you don't know it,' she said. Then she lied: 'He's gone now; gone out west.'

'Was it—' naming one or two.

'You never knew him. He came by the ranch on his way out west.'

Then she burst out crying, again, and he took her in his arms.

'It will be all over town,' said the mother-in-law. 'That girl made a fool of you.'

She slammed the dishes on the table and would have made the girl eat out the back door, but the young husband laid her a place at table with his own hands and led her in and sat her down in spite of his mother's black looks. They bowed their heads for grace. Surely, the Minister thought, seeing his boy cut bread for Annie-Belle and lay it on her plate, my son is a saint. He began to fear for him.

'I won't do anything unless you want,' her husband said in the dark after the candle went out.

The straw with which the mattress was stuffed rustled beneath her as she turned away from him.

> INTERIOR. FARMHOUSE KITCHEN. NIGHT.
> Johnny comes in from outside, looks at Father asleep in rocking chair.
> Picks up some discarded garment of Annie-Belle's from the back of a chair, buries face in it.
> Shoulders shake.

Opens cupboard, takes out bottle.
Uncorks with teeth. Drinks.
Bottle in hand, goes out on porch.

EXTERIOR. PRAIRIE. NIGHT.
JOHNNY'S POINT OF VIEW: Moon rising over prairie;
the vast, the elegiac plain.
'Landscape Theme' rises.

INTERIOR. MINISTER'S SON'S ROOM. NIGHT.
Annie-Belle and Minister's son in bed. Moonlight
through curtains. Both lie there, open-eyed. Rustle
of mattress.

ANNIE-BELLE: You awake?

Minister's son moves away from her.

ANNIE-BELLE: Reckon I never properly knowed no
    young man before . . .

MINISTER'S SON: What about—

ANNIE-BELLE: [*shrugging the question off*] Oh . . .

Minister's son moves towards her.

For she did not consider her brother in this new category of
'young men'; he was herself. So she and her husband slept in one
another's arms, that night, although they did nothing else for she
was scared it might harm the baby and he was so full of pain and
glory it was scarcely to be borne, it was already enough, or too
much, holding her tight, in his terrible innocence.

It was not so much that she was pliant. Only, fearing the worst,
it turned out that the worst had already happened; her sin found her
out, or, rather, she found out she had sinned only when he offered
his forgiveness, and, from her repentance, a new Annie-Belle
sprang up, for whom the past did not exist.

She would have said to him: it did not signify, my darling; I only
did it with my brother, we were alone together under the vast sky
that made us scared and so we clung together and what happened,
happened. But she knew she must not say that, that the most natural

191

thing of all was just precisely the one she must not acknowledge. To lie down on the prairie with a passing stranger was one thing. To lie down with her father's son was another. So she kept silent. And when she looked at her husband, she saw, not herself, but someone who might, in time, grow even more precious.

The next night, in spite of the baby, they did it, and his mother wanted to murder her and refused to get the breakfast for this prostitute, but Annie-Belle served them, put on an apron, cut the ham and cooked it, then scrubbed the floor with such humility, such evidence of gratitude that the older woman kept her mouth shut, her narrow lips tight as a trap but she kept them shut for if there was one thing she feared, it was the atrocious gentleness of her menfolk. And. So.

Johnny came to the town, hungering after her; the gates of Paradise slammed shut in his face. He haunted the backyard of the Minister's house, hid in the sweet-brier, watched the candle in their room go out and still he could not imagine it, that she might do it with another man. But. She did.

At the store, all gossip ceased when she came in; all eyes turned towards her. The old men chewing tobacco spat brown streams when she walked past. The women's faces veiled with disapproval. She was so young, so unaccustomed to people. They talked, her husband and she; they would go, just go, out west, still further, west as far as the place where the ocean starts again, perhaps. With his schooling, he could get some clerking job or other. She would bear her child and he would love it. Then she would bear *their* children.

Yes, she said. We shall do that, she said.

> EXTERIOR. FARMHOUSE. DAY.
> Annie-Belle drives up in trap.
> Johnny comes out on porch, in shirt-sleeves, bottle in hand.
> Takes her reins. But she doesn't get down from the trap.
>
> ANNIE-BELLE: Where's Daddy?
>
> Johnny gestures towards the prairie.

ANNIE-BELLE: [*not looking at Johnny*] Got something to tell him.

CLOSE-UP: Johnny.

JOHNNY: Ain't you got nothing to tell me?

CLOSE-UP: Annie-Belle.

ANNIE-BELLE: Reckon I ain't.

CLOSE-UP: Johnny.

JOHNNY: Get down and visit a while, at least.

CLOSE-UP: Annie-Belle.

ANNIE-BELLE: Can't hardly spare the time.

CLOSE-UP: Johnny and Annie-Belle.

JOHNNY: Got to scurry back, get your husband's dinner, is that it?

ANNIE-BELLE: Johnny . . . why haven't you come to church since I got married, Johnny?

Johnny shrugs, turns away.

EXTERIOR. FARMHOUSE. DAY.
Annie-Belle gets down from trap, follows Johnny towards farmhouse.

ANNIE-BELLE: Oh, Johnny, you *knowed* we did wrong.

Johnny walks towards farmhouse.

ANNIE-BELLE: I count myself fortunate to have found forgiveness.

JOHNNY: What are you going to tell Daddy?

ANNIE-BELLE: I'm going out west.

GIOVANNI: What, chang'd so soon! hath your new sprightly lord
Found out a trick in night-games more than we

Could know in our simplicity?—Ha! is't so?
Or does the fit come on you, to prove treacherous
To your past vows and oaths?

ANNABELLA: Why should you jest
At my calamity.

> EXTERIOR. FARMHOUSE. DAY.
>
> JOHNNY: Out west?
>
> Annie-Belle nods.
>
> JOHNNY: By yourself?
>
> Annie-Belle shakes her head.
>
> JOHNNY: With him?
>
> Annie-Belle nods.
> Johnny puts hand on porch rail, bends forward, hiding his face.
>
> ANNIE-BELLE: It is for the best.
>
> She puts her hand on his shoulder. He reaches out for her. She extricates herself. His hand, holding bottle; contents of bottle run out on grass.
>
> ANNIE-BELLE: It was wrong, what we did.
>
> JOHNNY: What about . . .
>
> ANNIE-BELLE: It shouldn't ever have been made, poor little thing. You won't never see it. Forget everything. You'll find yourself a woman, you'll marry.
>
> Johnny reaches out and clasps her roughly to him.

No, she said; never. No. And fought and bit and scratched: never! It's wrong. It's a sin. But, worse than that, she said: I don't want to, and she meant it, she knew she must not or else her new life, that lay before her, now, with the radiant simplicity of a child's drawing of a house, would be utterly destroyed. So she got free of

194

him and ran to the buggy and drove back lickety-split to town, beating the pony round the head with the whip.

Accompanied by a black trunk like a coffin, the Minister and his wife drove with them to a railhead such as you have often seen on the movies—the same telegraph office, the same water-tower, the same old man with the green eye-shade selling tickets. Autumn was coming on. Annie-Belle could no longer conceal her pregnancy, out it stuck; her mother-in-law could not speak to her directly but addressed remarks through the Minister, who compensated for his wife's contempt by showing Annie-Belle all the honour due to a repentant sinner.

She wore a yellow ribbon. Her hair was long and yellow. The repentant harlot has the surprised look of a pregnant virgin.

She is pale. The pregnancy does not go well. She vomits all morning. She bleeds a little. Her husband holds her hand tight. Her father came last night to say goodbye to her; he looks older. He does not take care of himself. That Johnny did not come set the tongues wagging; the gossip is, he refuses to set eyes on his sister in her disgrace. That seems the only thing to explain his attitude. All know he takes no interest in girls himself.

'Bless you, children,' says the Minister. With that troubling air of incipient sainthood, the young husband settles his wife down on the trunk and tucks a rug round her legs for a snappy wind drives dust down the railroad track and the hills are October mauve and brown. In the distance, the train whistle blows, that haunting sound, blowing across endless distance, the sound that underlines the distance.

> EXTERIOR. FARMHOUSE. DAY.
> Johnny mounts horse. Slings rifle over shoulder. Kicks horse's sides.
>
> EXTERIOR. RAILROAD. DAY.
> Train whistle. Burst of smoke.
> Engine pulling train across prairie.
>
> EXTERIOR. PRAIRIE. DAY.
> Johnny galloping down track.

EXTERIOR. RAILROAD. DAY.

CLOSE-UP: Train wheels turning.

EXTERIOR. PRAIRIE. DAY.

Hooves churning dust.

EXTERIOR. STATION. DAY.

MINISTER'S WIFE: Now, you take care of yourself, you hear? And—[but she can't bring herself to say it]

MINISTER: Be sure to tell us about the baby as soon as it comes.

CLOSE-UP: Annie-Belle smiling gratefully.
Train whistle.

And see them, now, as if posing for the photographer, the young man and the pregnant woman, sitting on a trunk, waiting to be transported onwards, away, elsewhere, she with the future in her belly.

EXTERIOR. STATION. DAY.
Station-master comes out of ticket-office.

STATION-MASTER: Here she comes!

LONG SHOT: Engine appearing round bend.

EXTERIOR. STATION. DAY.
Johnny tethers his horse.

ANNIE-BELLE: Why, Johnny, you've come to say goodbye after all!

CLOSE-UP: Johnny, wracked with emotion.

JOHNNY: He shan't have you. He'll never have you. Here's where you belong, with me. Out here.

GIOVANNI: Thus die, and die by me, and by my hand!
Revenge is mine; honour doth love command!

ANNABELLA: Oh, brother, by your hand!

EXTERIOR. STATION. DAY.

ANNIE-BELLE: Don't shoot—think of the baby! Don't—

MINISTER'S SON: Oh, my God—

Bang, bang, bang.

Thinking to protect his wife, the young husband threw his arms around her and so he died, by a split second, before the second bullet pierced her and both fell to the ground as the engine wheezed to a halt and passengers came tumbling off to see what Wild West antics were being played out while the parents stood and stared and did not believe, did not believe.

Seeing some life left in his sister, Johnny sank to his knees beside her and her eyes opened up and, perhaps, she saw him, for she said:

ANNABELLA: Brother, unkind, unkind . . .

So that Death would be well-satisfied, Johnny then put the barrel of the rifle into his mouth and pulled the trigger.

> EXTERIOR. STATION. DAY.
> Crane shot, the three bodies, the Minister comforting his wife, the passengers crowding off the train in order to look at the catastrophe.
>
> The 'Love Theme' rises over a pan of the prairie under the vast sky, the green breast of the continent, the earth, beloved, cruel, unkind.

Note: The Old World John Ford made Giovanni cut out Annabella's heart and carry it on stage; the stage direction reads: *Enter Giovanni, with a heart upon his dagger.* The New World John Ford would have no means of representing this scene on celluloid, although it is irresistibly reminiscent of the ritual tortures practised by the Indians who lived here before.

DON DELILLO
THE
IVORY ACROBAT

When it was over she stood in the crowded street and listened to the dense murmur of all those people speaking. She heard the first distant blurt of car horns on the avenue. People studied each other to match reactions. She watched them search the street for faces, signs that so-and-so was safe. She realized the street-lights were on and tried to recall how long her flat had been dark. Everyone was talking. She heard the same phrases repeated and stood with her arms crossed on her chest, watching a woman carry a chair to a suitable spot. The sound of blowing horns drifted through the streets. People leaving the city in radial streams. Already she was thinking ahead to the next one. There's always supposed to be another, possibly many more. The card-players stood outside the café, some of them inspecting a chunk of fallen masonry on the sidewalk, others looking towards the roof. Here and there a jutting face, a body slowly turning, searching. She wore what she'd been wearing when it started, jeans and shirt and light sweater, and it was night and winter, and funny-looking moccasins she only wore indoors. The horns grew louder in a kind of cry, an animal awe. The panic god is Greek after all. She thought about it again and wasn't sure the lights had been out at all. Women stood with arms folded in the cold. She walked along the middle of the street, listening to the voices, translating phrases to herself. It was the same for everyone. They said the same things and searched for faces. The streets were narrow here and people sat in parked cars, smoking. Here and there a child running, hand-shuffling through the crowd, excited children out near midnight. She thought there might be a glow in the sky and climbed a broad stepped street that had a vantage towards the gulf. She seemed to recall reading there's sometimes a light in the sky just before it happens or just after. This came under the heading of unexplained.

After a while they started going back inside. Kyle walked for three hours. She watched the cars push into major avenues that led to the mountains and the coast. Traffic-lights were dark in certain areas. The long lines of cars knotted and bent, made scant gains forward. Paralysis. She thought the scene resembled some landscape in the dreaming part of us, what the city teaches us to fear. They were pressing on the horns. The noise spread along the streets and reached a final mass denial, a desolation. It subsided after a time, then began to build again. She saw people sleeping on benches and families collected in cars parked on sidewalks and median strips. She recalled all the things she'd ever heard about an earthquake.

In her district the streets were almost empty now. She went into her building and took the stairs to five. The lights were on in her flat, and there were broken pieces of terracotta (she only now remembered) scattered on the floor by the bookcase. Long cracks branched along the west wall. She changed into walking shoes, put on a padded ski-jacket and turned off the lights except for a lamp by the door. Then she placed herself on the sofa between a sheet and blanket, her head resting on an airline pillow. She closed her eyes and folded up, elbows at her mid-section, hands pressed together between her knees. She tried to will herself to sleep but realized she was listening intently, listening to the room. She lay in a kind of timeless drift, a mindwork spiral, carried on half-formed thoughts. She passed into a false sleep and then was listening again. She opened her eyes. The clock read four-forty. She heard something that sounded like sand spilling, a trickle of gritty dust between the walls of abutting structures. The room began to move in a creaking sigh. Louder, powerfully. She was out of bed and on her way to the door, moving slightly crouched. She opened the door and stood under the lintel until the shaking stopped. She took the stairway down. No neighbours popping out of doors this time, bending arms into coats. The streets remained nearly empty and she guessed people didn't want to bother doing it again. She wandered well past daybreak. A few camp-fires burned in the parks. The horn-blowing was sporadic now. She walked around her building a number of times, finally sitting on a bench near the newspaper kiosk. She watched people enter the street to begin the day and she looked for something in their faces that might tell her what kind of night they'd spent. She was afraid everything would appear to be normal. She hated to think that people might easily resume the knockabout routine of frazzled Athens. She didn't want to be alone in her perception that something had basically changed. The world was narrowed down to inside and outside.

She had lunch with Edmund, a colleague at the little school where she taught music to children of the international community, grades three to six. She was eager to hear how he'd reacted to the situation but first talked him into eating outdoors at a table set against the façade of a busy snack-shop.

'We could still be killed,' Edmund said, 'by falling balconies. Or freeze in our chairs.'

'How did you feel?'

'I thought my heart was going to jump right through my chest.'

'Good. Me too.'

'I fled.'

'Of course.'

'On my way down the stairs I had the oddest conversation with the man who lives across the hall. I mean we'd hardly said a word to each other before this. There were two dozen people barrelling down the stairs. Suddenly he wanted to talk. He asked me where I work. Introduced me to his wife, who was pretty goddamn uninterested at that point in the details of my employment. He asked me how I like living in Greece.'

Skies were low and grey. People called to each other on the street, chanted from passing cars. *Eksi komma eksi.* They were referring to the first one, the bigger one. Six point six. Kyle had been hearing the number all morning, spoken with reverence, anxiety, grim pride, an echo along the brooding streets, a form of fatalistic greeting.

'Then what?' she said.

'The second one. I woke up moments before.'

'You heard something.'

'Like a child tossing a handful of sand against the window.'

'Very good,' she said.

'Then it hit.'

'It hit.'

'Bang. I leapt out of bed like a madman.'

'Did the lights go out?'

'No.'

'What about the first time?'

'I'm not sure actually.'

'Good. Neither am I. Was there a glow in the sky at any point?'

'Not that I noticed.'

'We could be dealing with a myth here.'

'The newspapers said a power-station may have failed, causing a flash. There's confusion on this point.'

'But we experienced similar things.'

'It would appear,' he said.

'Good. I'm glad.'

She thought of him as the English Boy although he was thirty-six, divorced, apparently arthritic and not even English. But he felt the English rapture over Greek light, where all Kyle saw was chemical smoke lapping at the ruins. And he had the prim outdated face of a schoolboy in a formal portrait, wire-haired and pensive.

'Where was the epicentre?' she said.

'About forty miles west of here.'

'The dead?'

'Thirteen and counting.'

'What will we do?'

'About what?' he said.

'Everything. All the after-shocks.'

'We've had 200 already. It's expected to last many weeks. Read the papers. Months perhaps.'

'Look, Edmund. I don't want to be alone tonight. OK?'

She lived inside a pause. She was always pausing, alone in her flat, to listen. Her hearing developed a cleanness, a discriminating rigour. She sat at the small table where she ate her meals, listening. The room had a dozen sounds, mainly disturbances of tone, pressures releasing in the walls, and she followed them and waited. There was a second and safer level she reserved for street noises, the elevator rising. All the danger was inside.

A rustle. A soft sway. She crouched in the open doorway like an atomic child.

The tremors entered her bloodstream. She listened and waited. She couldn't sleep at night and caught odd moments in daytime, dozing in an unused room at school. She dreaded going home. She watched the food in her plate and sometimes stood, carefully listening, ready to go, to get outside. There must be something funny in this somewhere, a person standing motionless over her food, leaning ever so slightly towards the door, fingertips at the table edge.

Is it true that before a major quake the dogs and cats run away? She thought she'd read somewhere that people in California habitually check the personal columns in newspapers to see if the number of lost dogs has increased noticeably. Or are we dealing with a myth here?

The wind made the shutters swing and bang. She listened to the edges of the room, the interfaces. She heard everything. She put a tote bag near the door for hasty exits—money, books, passport, letters from home. She heard the sound of the knife-sharpener's bell.

She didn't read the papers but gathered that the tremors numbered in the 800s by latest count and the dead added up to twenty now, with hotel rubble and tent cities near the epicentre and people living in open areas in parts of Athens, their buildings judged unsafe.

The card-players wore their coats indoors. She walked past the cut-back mulberry trees and through the street market and looked at the woman selling eggs and wondered what she could say to her that might make them both feel better, in her fairly decent Greek, shopping for bargains. A man held the elevator door, but she waved him off politely and took the stairs. She walked into her flat, listening. The terrace canopies humped out in the wind, snapping hard. She wanted her life to be episodic again, unpremeditated. A foreigner anonymous—soft-footed, self-informed, content to occupy herself in random observation. She wanted to talk unimportantly to grandmothers and children in the streets of her working-class district.

She rehearsed her exit mentally. So many steps from the table to the door. So many stairs to the street. She thought if she pictured it beforehand, it might go more smoothly.

The lottery man cried, 'Today, today.'

She tried to read through the edgy nights, the times of dull-witted terror. There were rumours that these were not after-shocks at all but warnings of some deep disquiet in the continental trench, the massing of a force that would roll across the marble-hearted city and bring it to dust. She sat up and turned the pages, trying to disguise herself as someone who routinely reads for fifteen minutes before dropping into easy sleep.

It was not so bad in school, where she was ready to protect the young, to cover their bodies with her own.

The tremors lived in her skin and were part of every breath she took. She paused over her food. A rustle. An easing reedy tilt. She stood and listened, alone with the shaking earth.

Edmund told her he'd bought a gift to replace the terracotta roof ornament she'd had propped against the wall above the bookcase, acanthus leaves radiating from the head of a sleepy-eyed Hermes, shattered in the first tremor.

'You won't miss your Hermes all that much. I mean it's everywhere, isn't it?'

'That's what I liked about it.'

'You can easily get another. They're piled up for sale.'

'It'll only get broken,' she said, 'when the next one hits.'

'Let's change the subject.'

'There's only one subject. That's the trouble. I used to have a personality. What am I now?'

'Try to understand it's over.'

'I'm down to pure dumb canine instinct.'

'Life is going on. People are going about their business.'

'No, they're not. Not the same way. Just because they don't walk around moaning.'

'There's nothing to moan about. It's finished.'

'Doesn't mean they're not preoccupied. It's been less than a week. There are tremors all the time.'

'Growing ever smaller,' he said.

'Some are not so small. Some are definite attention-getters.'

'Change the subject please.'

They were standing just outside the school entrance, and Kyle was watching a group of children climb aboard a bus for a trip to a museum outside the city. She knew she could count on the English Boy to be exasperated with her. He was dependable that way. She always knew the position he would take and could often anticipate the actual words, practically moving her lips in unison with his. He brought some stability to dire times.

'You used to be lithe.'

'Look at me now,' she said.

'Lumbering.'

'I wear layers of clothing. I wear clothes and change-of-clothes simultaneously. Just to be ready.'

'I can't afford a change of clothes,' he said.

'I can't afford the dry cleaning.'

'I often wonder how this happened to me.'

'I live without a refrigerator and telephone and radio and shower-curtain and what else. I keep butter and milk on the balcony.'

'You're very quiet,' he said then. 'Everyone says so.'

'Am I? Who?'

'How old are you by the way?'

'Now that we've spent a night together, you mean?'

'Spent a night. Exactly. One night used up in huddled conversation.'

'Well it helped me. It made a difference really. It was the crucial night. Not that the others have been so cosy.'

'You're welcome to return, you know. I sit there thinking. A lithe young woman flying across the city into my arms.'

The children waved at them from the windows, and Edmund did a wild-eyed mime of a bus driver caught in agitated traffic. She watched the lightsome faces glide away.

'You have nice colour,' she said.

'What does that mean?'

'Your cheeks are pink and healthy. My father used to say if I ate my vegetables I'd have rosy cheeks.'

She waited for Edmund to ask, 'What did your mother used to say?' Then they walked for the time that remained before afternoon classes. Edmund bought a ring of sesame bread and gave her half. He paid for things by opening his fist and letting the vendor sort among the coins. It proved to everyone that he was only passing through.

'You've heard the rumours,' she said.

'Rubbish.'

'The government is concealing seismic data.'

'There is absolutely no scientific evidence that a great quake is imminent. Read the papers.'

She took off the bulky jacket and swung it over her shoulder. She realized she wanted him to think she was slightly foolish, controlled by mass emotion. There was some comfort in believing the worst as long as this was the reigning persuasion. But she didn't want to submit completely. She walked along wondering if she was appealing to Edmund for staunch pronouncements that she could use against herself.

'Do you have an inner life?'

'I sleep,' he said.

'That's not what I mean.'

They ran across a stretch of avenue where cars accelerated to a racing clip. It felt good to shake out of her jittery skin. She kept running for half a block and then turned to watch him approach clutching his chest and moving on doddery legs, as if for the regalement of children. He could look a little bookish even capering.

They approached the school building.

'I wonder what your hair would be like if you let it grow out.'

'I can't afford the extra shampoo,' she said.

'I can't afford a haircut at regular intervals, quite seriously.'

'I live without a piano.'

'And this is a wretchedness to compare with no refrigerator?'

'You can ask that question because you don't know me. I live without a bed.'

'Is this true?'

'I sleep on a second-hand sofa. It has the texture of a barnacled hull.'

'Then why stay?' he said.

'I can't save enough to go anywhere else and I'm certainly not ready to go home. Besides I like it here. I'm sort of stranded but in a more or less willing way. At least until now. The trouble with now is that we could be anywhere. The only thing that matters is where we're standing when it hits.'

He presented the gift then, lifting it out of his jacket pocket and unwrapping the sepia paper with a teasing show of suspense. It was a reproduction of an ivory figurine from Crete, a bull-leaper, female, her body deftly extended with tapered feet nearing the topmost point of a somersaulting curve. Edmund explained that the young woman was in the act of vaulting over the horns of a charging bull. This was a familiar scene in Minoan art, found in frescoes, bronzes, clay seals, gold signet rings, ceremonial cups. Most often a young man, sometimes a woman gripping a bull's horns and swinging up and over, propelled by the animal's head-jerk. He told her the original ivory figure was broken in half in 1926 and asked her if she wanted to know how this happened.

'Don't tell me. I want to guess.'

'An earthquake. But the restoration was routine.'

Kyle took the figure in her hand.

'A bull coming at full gallop? Is this possible?'

'I'm not inclined to question what was possible 3,600 years ago.'

'I don't know the Minoans,' she said. 'Were they that far back?'

'Yes, and farther than that, much farther.'

'Maybe if the bull was firmly tethered.'

'It's never shown that way,' he said. 'It's shown big and fierce and running and bucking.'

'Do we have to believe something happened exactly the way it was shown by artists?'

'No. But I believe it. And even though this particular leaper isn't accompanied by a bull, we know from her position that this is what she's doing.'

'She's bull-leaping.'

'Yes.'

'And she will live to tell it.'

'She has lived. She is living. That's why I got this for you really. I want her to remind you of your hidden litheness.'

'But you're the acrobat,' Kyle said. 'You're the loose-jointed one, performing in the streets.'

'To remind you of your fluent buoyant former self.'

'You're the jumper and heel-clicker.'

'My joints ache like hell actually.'

'Look at the veins in her hand and arm.'

'I got it cheap in the flea market.'

'That makes me feel much better.'

'It's definitely you,' he said. 'It must be you. Do we agree on this? Just look and feel. It's your magical true self, mass-produced.'

Kyle laughed.

'Lean and supple and young,' he said. 'Throbbing with inner life.'

She laughed. Then the school bell rang and they went inside.

She stood in the middle of the room, dressed except for shoes, slowly buttoning her blouse. She paused. She worked the button through the slit. Then she stood on the wood floor, listening.

They were now saying twenty-five dead, thousands homeless. Some people had abandoned undamaged buildings, preferring the ragged safety of life outdoors. Kyle could easily see how that might happen. She had the first passable night's sleep but continued to stay off elevators and out of movie theatres. The wind knocked loose objects off the back balconies. She listened and waited. She visualized her exit from the room.

Sulphur fell from the factory skies, staining the pavement, and a teacher at the school said it was sand blown north from Libya on one of those lovely desert winds.

She sat on the sofa in pyjamas and socks reading a book on local flora. A blanket covered her legs. A half-filled glass of water sat on the end table. Her eyes wandered from the page. It was two minutes before midnight. She paused, looking off towards the middle distance. Then she heard it coming, an earth-roar, a power moving on the air. She sat for a long second, deeply thoughtful, before throwing off the blanket. The moment burst around her. She rushed to the door and opened it, half aware of rattling lampshades and something wet. She gripped the edges of the door-frame and faced into the room. Things were jumping up and down. She formed the categorical thought: *This one is the biggest yet.* The room was more or less a blur. There was a sense that it was on the verge of splintering. She felt the effect in her legs this time, a kind of hollowing out, a soft surrender to some illness. It was hard to believe, hard to believe it was lasting so long. She pushed her hands against the door-frame, searching for a calmness in herself. She could almost see a picture of her mind, a vague grey oval, floating over the room. The shaking would not stop. There was an anger in it, a hammering demand. Her face showed the crumpled effort of a heavy lifter. It wasn't easy to know what was happening around her. She couldn't see things in the normal way. She could only see herself, bright-skinned, waiting for the room to fold over her.

Then it ended and she pulled some clothes over her pyjamas and took the stairway down. She moved fast. She ran across the small lobby, brushing past a man lighting a cigarette at the door. People were coming into the street. She went half a block and stopped at the edge of a large group. She was breathing hard and her arms hung limp. Her first clear thought was that she'd have to go back inside sooner or later. She listened to the voices fall around her. She wanted to hear someone say this very thing, that the cruelty existed in time, that they were all unprotected in the drive of time. She told a woman she thought a water-pipe had broken in her flat and the woman closed her eyes and rocked her heavy head. When will it all end? She told the woman she'd forgotten to grab her tote bag on her way out the door despite days of careful planning and she tried to give the story a rueful nuance, make it funny and faintly self-mocking. There must be something funny we can cling to. They stood there rocking their heads.

All up and down the street there were people lighting cigarettes. It was eight days since the first tremor, eight days and one hour.

She walked most of the night. At three a.m. she stopped in the square in front of the Olympic Stadium. There were parked cars and scores of people and she studied the faces and stood listening. Traffic moved slowly past. There was a curious double mood, a lonely reflectiveness at the centre of all the talk, a sense that people were half-absent from the eager seeking of company. She started walking again.

Eating breakfast in her flat at nine o'clock she felt the first sizeable after-shock. The room leaned heavily. She rose from the table, eyes wet, and opened the door and crouched there, holding a buttered roll.

Wrong. The last one was not the biggest on the Richter. It was only six point two.

And she found out it hadn't lasted longer than the others. This was a mass illusion, according to the word at school.

And the water she'd seen or felt had not come from a broken pipe but from a toppled drinking-glass on the table by the sofa.

And why did they keep occurring at night?

And where was the English Boy?

The drinking-glass was intact but her paperback book on plant life was wet and furrowed.

She took the stairs up and down.

She kept the tote bag ready at the door.

She was deprived of sentiments, pretensions, expectations, textures.

The pitiless thing was time, threat of advancing time.

She was deprived of presumptions, persuasions, complications, lies, every braided arrangement that made it possible to live.

Stay out of movies and crowded halls. She was down to categories of sound, to self-admonishments and endless inner scrutinies.

She paused, alone, to listen.

She pictured her sensible exit from the room.

She looked for something in people's faces that might tell her their experience was just like hers, down to the smallest strangest turn of thought.

There must be something funny in this somewhere that we can use to get us through the night.

She heard everything.

She took catnaps at school.

She was deprived of the city itself. We could be anywhere, any lost corner of Ohio.

She dreamed of a mayfly pond skimmed with fallen blossoms.

Take the stairs everywhere. Take a table near the exit in cafés and tavernas.

The card-players sat in hanging smoke, making necessary motions only, sombrely guarding their cards.

She learned that Edmund was in the north with friends, peering into monasteries.

She heard the surge of motorcycles on the hill.

She inspected the cracks in the west wall and spoke to the landlord, who closed his eyes and rocked his heavy head.

The wind caused a rustling somewhere very near.

She sat up at night with her book of water-stiffened pages, trying to read, trying to escape the feeling that she was being carried helplessly towards some pitching instant in time.

The acanthus is a spreading perennial.

And everything in the world is either inside or outside.

She came across the figurine one day inside a desk drawer at school, lying among cough-drops and paper-clips, in an office used as a teachers' lounge. She didn't even remember putting it there and felt the familiar clashing agencies of shame and defensiveness working in her blood—a body heat rising against the reproach of forgotten things. She picked it up, finding something remarkable in the leaper's clean and open motion, in the detailed tension of forearms and hands. Shouldn't something so old have a formal bearing, a stiffness of figure? This was easy-flowing work. But beyond this surprise, there was little to know. She didn't know the Minoans. She wasn't even sure what the thing was made of, what kind of lightweight imitation ivory. It occurred to her that she'd left the figure in the desk because she didn't know what to do with it, how to underpin or prop it. The body was alone in space, with no supports, no fixed position, and seemed best suited to the palm of the hand.

She stood in the small room, listening.

Edmund had said the figure was like her. She studied it, trying to extract the sparest recognition. A girl in a loincloth and wristbands, double-necklaced, suspended over the horns of a running bull. The act, the leap itself, might be vaudeville or sacred terror. There were themes and secrets and storied lore in this six-inch figure that Kyle could not begin to guess at. She turned the object in her hand. All the facile parallels fell away. Lithe, young, buoyant, modern; rumbling bulls and quaking earth. There was nothing that might connect her to the mind inside the work, an ivory-carver, 1600 B.C., moved by forces remote from her. She remembered the old earthen Hermes, flower-crowned, looking out at her from a knowable past, some shared theatre of being. The Minoans were outside all this. Narrow-waisted, graceful, other-minded—lost across vales of language and magic, across dream cosmologies. This was the piece's little mystery. It was a thing in opposition, defining what she was not, marking the limits of the self. She closed her fist around it firmly and thought she could feel it beat against her skin with a soft and periodic pulse, an earthliness.

She was motionless, with tilted head, listening. Buses rolled past, sending diesel fumes through seams in the window frame. She looked towards a corner of the room, concentrating tightly. She listened and waited.

Her self-awareness ended where the acrobat began. Once she realized this, she put the object in her pocket and took it everywhere.

JOHN BERGER
MEANS OF
TRANSPORT

John Berger

To learn how to speak
With the voices of this land.
Jeremy Cronin

Use these photos as means of transport. Ride on them. No passes needed. Go close. Imprudently close. They leave every minute. Their drivers are there on the spot—often at considerable risk to their cameras and themselves. But we who are travelling risk nothing—except a reminder that justice has to be fought for, that often it has to be fought for, generation after generation, against men armed to the teeth and against men, there where the photos take us, who have even manufactured a nuclear bomb to defend their wicked white power. Go close.

The statistics inevitably have to be calibrated from afar. Four-fifths of the population there—that is to say over twenty-five million souls—have no vote. Continually displaced, they do not have the right to live or work where they choose. Under the apartheid laws they are restricted to thirteen per cent of the poorest land, the so-called 'bantustans', where economic survival is impossible. Those who leave to try to earn a living for their families become—unless they have a temporary contract—illegal immigrants in their own country. Many in the shanty towns on the edges of the cities remain unemployed. Those who do get work constitute one of the most exploited industrial labour forces in the world.

The white minority have an average life expectancy of 73.9 years: the four-fifths majority a life expectancy of 59.8 years. In the country of the first heart transplant, 50,000 black children die every year from malnutrition. But hunger, comes the evil reply, is endemic to Africa! Last year in South Africa more than 2,000 children were imprisoned with their mothers. Is imprisonment too endemic to Africa? Take the photos and go close. Imprudently close.

Women and men come to the doors of the shacks where they live. They look at the camera. They look at us visiting. They are sombre. On one shoulder a man carries the weight of the past, on the other his child. Beyond all the universities in the world these women and their children and men embody history. And they know it.

Photo: Jenny Gordon

214

Love life. Be like the sunlight afforded this earth and love life. Not because life in this prison state of apartheid is lovable, but simply because all that is lovable comes from life. Get down at Crossroads, the squatter-camp near Cape Town. Everyone is there illegally. Their homes will be burnt down. The land will be cleared. They will be evicted, driven out, beaten up. They have nowhere to go. On nowhere they built homes. Look at their children. Like children everywhere they have been given a name. Unlike children in most places, many will also be given a number soon, a number on the police computers. See. Their parents have given them space, the space to be themselves within their name; they are loved. Parents who don't have a single square metre to sit down upon or to call their own have given their children space. The *Casspirs*, the riot vehicles, can't evict from the heart. Here the *Casspirs* are powerless.

Marx's vision that the proletariat would become increasingly impoverished and exploited until it had nothing to lose but its chains and that the capitalists would become increasingly and disproportionately wealthy has been proved false in all the industrialized countries of the world, except South Africa. Here his prophecy is being realized. What Marx couldn't foresee was that the proletariat would be black and the capitalists white. Ineradicably true.

Photo: Paul Weinberg

In a home, made of tarpaulin and corrugated iron and wrapping
paper, a broom leans against a wall, and the woman of the
house, built on nowhere, will take it to sweep.

In an official barrack built for migrant workers, hundreds or
thousands of miles away from home, of women there is only talk.
Between the single bunks the promise of normal family life is like
coconut milk in a hand-grenade.

Yes, there is resistance. And fear too. How could there not be
fear? Better to ask when getting down at the barracks: how to live
with fear and sometimes overcome it?

In the new coffins of the newly assassinated there are young
bodies but also the entire history whose weight is on every black

shoulder. At the funerals the words: BULLETS WON'T STOP US are written. When the young believe in what they have seen and live this belief, their beauty makes them unstoppable.

More can be shot dead of course. But then, as martyrs, their beauty becomes immortal.

None of this for one instant diminishes the pain of the whip or the grief of the mother or the despair of the mutilated. Not for a single instant.

> The stormtroopers are in the streets
> the women wash dishes with their tears.
> Hein Willemse

John Berger

Come closer. Reckoning consequences and the rules of cause and effect belongs to a calculation that cannot be found here. Here there is nothing to the future except hope. That hope is beautiful. But apart from this hope, the future is already devastated, a continuation of the catastrophe of the past whose weight is on every shoulder. Here there can be no consequences as calculated elsewhere. Only hope and her brother fear. And this—which is hard for visitors to understand—is why the kids write and will go on writing: BULLETS WON'T STOP US.

Get down now at one of the military parades. Those in the uniforms are damned. This is visible in their faces. Without hope, with nothing but their weapons and murderous orders, their faces have shrunk to resemble the hams of pigs. Watch. They have everything. The wealth of the country, bullet-proof protection, property, homes, united families, servants, bank accounts, beaches, yachts, a life expectancy of seventy-four—and they have no hope. If it happens that they love somebody, all they can offer their loved one is to take their weapon, load it and wait. They own everything and hope has abandoned them. They have all become their own henchmen, yet today there is no one left for the henchmen to protect. The ruling class has become the killing class.

The killing class can't sing. The homeless do.

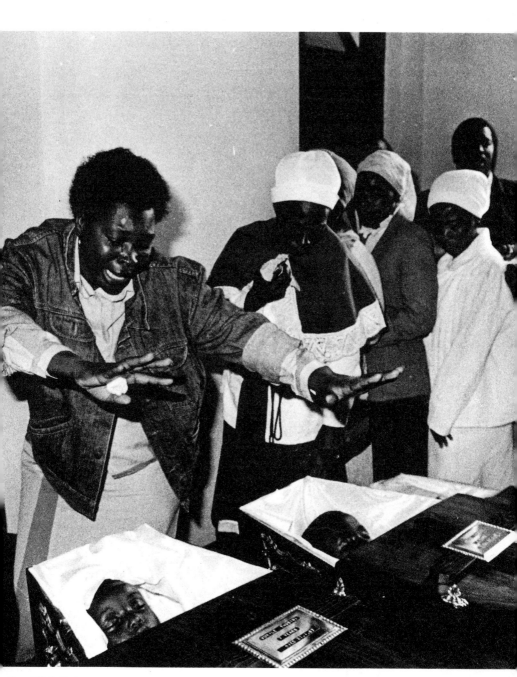

Photo: Billy Paddock

Photo: Paul Grendon

Lady Day, Lady Day,
Lady Day of no happy days,
Who lives in a voice
Sagging with the pain
Where the monster's teeth
Are deep to our marrow.
    Keoropetse Kgositsee

The killing class print out lies and make up new legal terms. They parrot. They curse. They issue orders. Yet the gift of words is a thing they can no longer acquire. And this is why they are frightened, not of lions or leopards or anything that can be shot, but of words.

Here is another squatters' camp outside Cape Town, which is the port of what the colonizers once called the Cape of Good Hope. The KTC camp. In a make-shift shelter a family on a bed. They have no work and no pass, which means that on this bed they are illegal. They have already been evicted from other 'shelters' thirty or forty times. The mother is wearing a Scottish plaid recalling other evictions in another country. Their shoes are arranged under the bed. A clean newspaper on the table. Cloths neatly folded. One has flowers printed on it. In this shelter, constructed from discarded packaging, a home has been improvised. They are not looking at their visitors. From them they expect nothing. They are remembering. Something else.

> The Ancestors invite us to the vision of the river.
> Knowing we have suffered enough;
> Through them we float aimlessly on a dream
> And yet our names must remain hidden from total joy
> Lest through weakness we may succumb
> Falling slowly into the depths of mindlessness,
> Our love must survive through the ancient flames.
> We must congregate here around the sitting mat,
> To narrate endlessly the stories of distant worlds.
> It is enough to do so,
> To give our tale the grandeur of an ancient heritage
> And then to clap our hands for those who are younger than us.
>
> Mazisi Kunene

The dead fight too. Their innocence is fighting the guilt of the killers. This guilt is such that the killing class cannot tolerate the colours of a flag which accuse them. Study the face of the officer of the riot police at Ashrey Kriel's funeral. The flag he is trying to tear off the coffin is that of the African National Congress. He believes that people can be torn up like paper. One day he will tear things up in his own home. Unlike the family in the KTC camp he can cherish nothing any more. He has lost the faculty. His hands can only grasp or wring.

Another funeral. This time in Lesotho, of ANC members killed during a police raid. The first mourner following the coffin is a white woman. She holds up her clenched fist. Her gesture is so vulnerable and yet it declares: resistance and victory. One of the

223

Photo: Gideon Mendel

pall-bearers is also a white woman. Go close. There is no reason for either of them to turn or hide. The secret police already have a complete dossier concerning them. According to these dossiers they are traitors to their race and country: they support terrorists; they consort with communists. Even the clothes of the pall-bearers confirm that she deserves to be a convict.

Please look at her face. She is grave. She is very close at this moment to her conscience. They are walking cheek to cheek. She has chosen another kind of homelessness. And on her left shoulder she has chosen to carry the weight of history. I hope I will never forget this photograph. It was taken in the future, on the far side of barbarism.

This is Mayfair railway station in Johannesburg. A group of miners are waiting for a train to take them home. Their twelve-month contract working for the gold companies is over. They have become illegal again. They look tired, cold, disoriented. These are the men who extract from the earth the very symbol of wealth, the magic substance of the alchemists. Their brothers do the same for diamonds. Facing them, we stare at what *hierarchy* means. Under the earth they are at the bottom, near disaster: what they produce goes exclusively to the top. The photo was taken more than thirty years ago.

In 1985 the Congress of South African Trade Unions was launched. It is the largest trade union body in Africa. In 1987 it adopted the Freedom Charter for democracy.

Visit a strike today. The workers are listening to a speech. They are an audience, seated, their eyes on a stage from which they are being addressed. Study their expressions more closely. Each one knows that they are the actors too and that an invisible audience is watching *them*. Among this second invisible audience are hired killers, spies, police-chiefs, informers. But also in this second audience are all the prisoners of history, waiting to break out. No single person can decide the day. The day will come.

The meaning of the word CHAIN will be changed into that which links and joins. Not by decree but by freely chosen action. 'An artist,' said John Muafangejo, an engraver from Namibia, 'is struggling with chains in order to tear them from the stem.' Tear them from the stem.

Stop at the concert in Alexandra township. The poet 'Jingles' is performing to drums. He is looking over an invisible wall which is everywhere. He's reminding people that on the other side of the wall the land stretches to the horizon. He's showing that one can speak over the wall and be heard. Soon after the concert 'Jingles' was assassinated by unknown gunmen. Here art is not protection.

A daughter touches the hand of her arrested father as he is shoved into a car to be carried off. Remember the gesture of her hand. It is one from which nothing can ever be torn away, for it accompanies, accompanies wordlessly in the disappearing car, in the cell, in the courtroom. At this instant of brutal separation, there is a joining by faith.

> Of course we never get to speak,
> As such, to each other.
> We're still fifty yards, one corridor,
> Many locked locks apart.
> Jeremy Cronin

Two young men, wearing Freedom Fighter T-shirts, cast their farewell earth into the grave of a killed comrade. Their heads are bowed, for the comrade has gone for ever and his likeness will never occur again. He is irretrievable. A terrible word when spoken with love. Yet the gestures of their hands throwing the dust are deliberate. One is holding the earth for the last time before casting. The second hand is straight and has cast. Both of them very deliberate. They know exactly what they are doing. They are joining the living and the dead so that their hopes, becoming the same, will be irrepressible.

For the transport back to where we live any publicity photo in any colour magazine will do. Express non-stop service. All classes. Dogs allowed. But no History.

JOHN STURROCK
MUIRHOUSE

They had seen journalists before, television crews mainly, who'd rush in, get what they wanted and disappear again. Inevitably the kids felt used. I didn't want to be another journalist.

I made several trips—whenever I got the chance between jobs—and would stay for three, four, maybe five days. It wasn't always the best setting for pictures, so much of the time we'd just talk. And then, after some time, they let me follow when they went off for a hit.

I was very distressed by what I saw. I had seen people shooting up before, but I had never seen anything like this. I hadn't expected them to begin shooting up in the groin. I had no idea of the physical problems they had, that their veins had become so hard, that *every* vein had become so hard from so many years of use that they just couldn't get the needle in. I had never seen self-abuse so extreme. Because I had got close to them, because I had to get close to them to be able to work with them—especially because I wasn't entirely sure what I was doing—I began to feel irritated by what they did to themselves. It was so self-defeating and so destructive, and the more I saw the more angry I felt. I never let them see the anger. In fact, in the face of everything I saw, I ended up shutting off most of my feelings. I was working on automatic, the person who takes the pictures, someone with a job to do. Later, when I got home, I found that I had an awful lot locked away. I had a terrible need to unclamp all of these feelings. I remember phoning friends or writing down thoughts on pieces of paper—anything that would help me feel. The other day I came across the back of an envelope on which I had described the events of the day:

Last year, the research of Roy Robertson, an Edinburgh doctor working with young drug-users at Muirhouse, a government-subsidized housing estate, attracted the attention of television and newspapers: he had discovered that many of the young drug-users were HIV-positive; some had already contracted AIDS. In January 1988, photographer John Sturrock made the first of five trips to the estate. This text is based on an extended interview.

'Leslie! Leslie!'

The big lad's shout is heartfelt. He bangs on the door. Inside we go quiet and I shrink into my chair. I've seen him before, in his thick, white jumper, jeans and brogues. And his pain. I don't know whether to fear or hug him. His emotions are displayed like entrails. They are all like that. Wasted bodies, childish behaviour, crushing me. I absorb it, like punishment, knowing that later it will haunt me.

He bangs on the door. She curses quietly and tells him to go away, she's trying to sleep, she'll see him later. He sighs and leaves us.

I know when I meet him next he will have heard that they had taken me to her room so that I could watch and photograph and that he was excluded. He'll know that I saw the woman he needed in her underclothes—hunched over, slowly puncturing her groin with a needle—with her companion, naked and triumphant, calling over to me, his blood-filled syringe hanging beside his penis.

When I left them—there in their cotton-wool, clogged euphoria—I stroked her face, telling her to take care. I felt stupid. And when the door closed behind me, I felt cold and hard, like the concrete buildings.

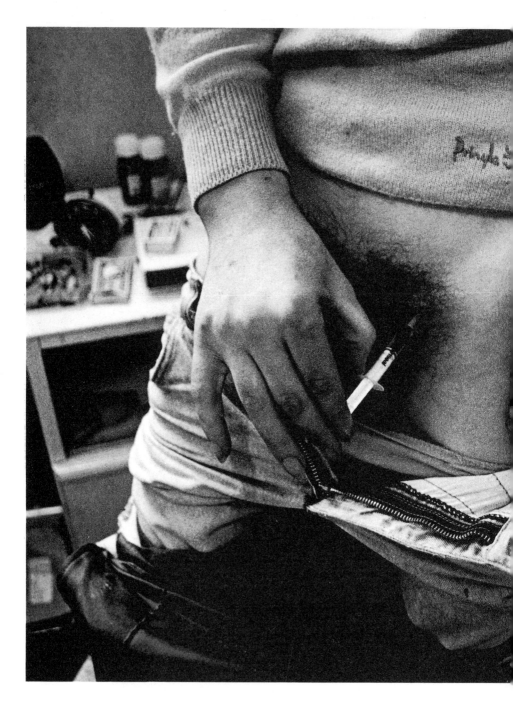

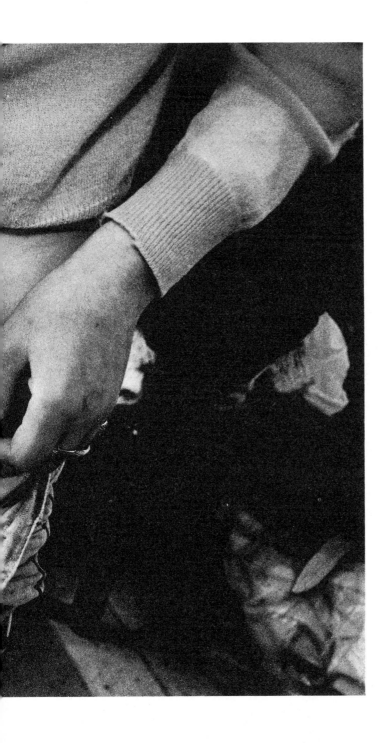

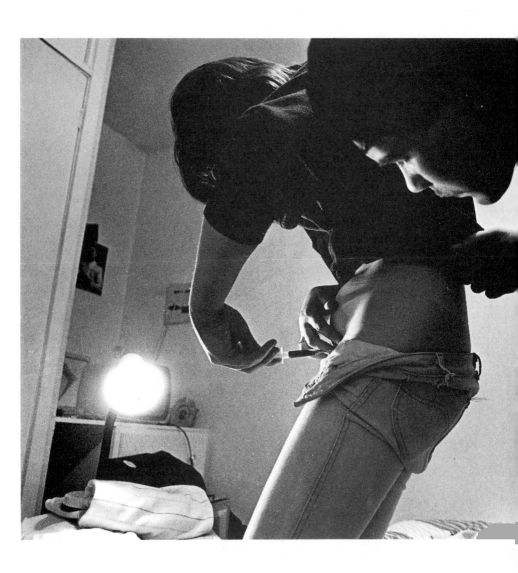

This was the procedure: they'd get a handful of capsules. I have no idea what was in them; there was all kinds of stuff around. And then they'd break open the capsules with a Stanley knife, filling the syringe with the liquid. Today there are sensible ones who have their own syringe and don't share, but some still do. They'd eat the bulk of the capsules and then start looking for a vein off which they could still get a hit. It was a matter of injecting and then drawing the syringe out, drawing out the blood, and then pushing it back, and then drawing it out again, over and over. They were all fixated on the needle. They were obsessed by the needle.

You forget how dangerous it is. At this point, though, I think he was actually concerned for her—there was a problem with the needle. They help each other, help each other to get a hit.

She used to take heroin—I don't know for how long, a long time, since leaving school—but there hasn't been any heroin around and she's a user of whatever she can get her hands on. She's twenty-two and is HIV-positive. She's trying to keep herself together by doing a number of very specific personal things. She washes her hair every day, for instance. That's important. It's an important ritual. She has changed her diet. She is concerned about personal hygiene. She is reading a book about massage and medication and the body. But she still takes drugs.

I don't want to put words in her mouth but I suppose I would characterize her attitude to her future as one of resignation. Her day consists of filling up time. The whole culture is one of filling up time. You've got to go out. You've got to get the drugs. You've got to see people, negotiate with them. You inject. It's very social. It's been known for years that in Edinburgh there is a habit of needle-sharing, for instance, which you'd never see in London. It's communal. And then, after a while, you've got to go out again. It's a full-time occupation.

But every day she washes her hair.

John Sturrock

I like this picture particularly because
of the normality of the fish-tank, the
picture on the wall, the flowers. The
house is reasonably clean. I got the
impression that if something was
spilled, he'd be over there wiping it up.
His girl-friend was in the room. She
wants him to give it up, but he won't.
He's not HIV-positive and that's a big
relief to her. He's a sweet character—
lively and funny, doing a lot but with
nothing to do. He's nineteen or twenty.

He was never concerned about my
being there. None of them were.
Maybe they had shot up before with
photographers. On one of my trips, I
returned with the pictures I had taken.
I had made a point all along of trying to
get some cheerful ones—sometimes I
had to work quite hard to get them
outside, smiling, looking attractive.
They liked those pictures very much.
But when I showed them the ones of
them shooting up, everything changed.
The room became very quiet. No one
said anything. It was a stunned silence;
they just kept looking at the pictures,
one after the other.

They're feeling pretty lousy. They've shot up a few times, but the last time was a while ago and they're ready for another. It's a cold, grey Edinburgh day. The estate—damp and concrete and grey—is a desolate place. It isolates people. Growing up there, it takes a lot even to imagine how you'll ever be able to leave it.

We went into town, into Edinburgh, on the bus. It was like taking a school party. All along Princes Street, you see nothing but the famous shops, and they all have security guards outside, even the smaller ones. The woman had just taken a hit. When they're high on drugs, they feel like they are some kind of superman—everything is possible. And so she believed it was possible simply to take anything that took her fancy. Edinburgh is grand and beautiful: coming from a council estate, it's like entering a foreign city. We went to a shop that was selling helium-filled balloons, big silver ones. She went up and took one and walked off with it. It was funny.

This picture is about a moment. The man in the leather jacket has just come out of prison. I'm not sure what for. Robbery, assault. Everyone is going in and out of prison. And this is the moment of reunion. It's jovial and chatty and witty, and then suddenly he lowers his face into his hands and groans. He could see that it was all about to start over again and he couldn't face it. And it would: soon they would go off together, they would buy drugs and they'd use them.

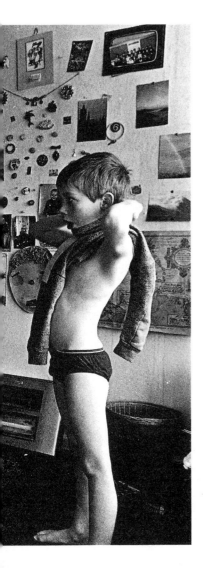

She was the one who appeared so many times on the television, having discovered that she was HIV-positive and yet still carrying on working as a prostitute. She was 'the AIDS carrier of Edinburgh' and was called that wherever she went. Always out of context. The hostility was enormous. And the boy has seen quite a bit of it as well. I spent the evening with her. It was painful watching her peel potatoes. It took her ages. Maybe it was because I was there. I can't tell. She was trying very hard to keep herself together. In fact that was why I liked spending time with her, because she was trying so hard to keep herself together. She had begun to control her life considerably. She was looking after herself.

The context of photo-journalism is usually provided by some kind of serious issue—war, crime, deprivation—but the pictures themselves are rarely about the issue: they're about the victims. I'm not interested in endless pictures of victims. There are always other people, people who are trying to comprehend the issue, hoping to overcome it, to get out, be free of it.

I had no idea what I would find at Muirhouse, but I did know that I did not want to have to do a story of victims. If a British newspaper had commissioned the story, it would be another shocking collection of horror shots. But I wanted to do something more: a context that would allow someone to understand the issue—not just the victims, but those trying to get out. What is the value of horror shots?

In the sixties, Don McCullin's photographs from the Vietnam War were shocking, but there was a purpose, a way of receiving those photographs: the protest movement at the time. But what makes me uneasy is that we have no way of receiving these pictures from Muirhouse. How do we interpret them? We're at a time of very low confidence. Most people will see these pictures and blame the people in them for their plight. It will be their fault. I don't believe that's right.

NOTES FROM ABROAD

Tibetan Dinner
Amitav Ghosh

I t was a while before the others at the table had finished pointing out the celebrities who had come to the restaurant for the gala benefit: the Broadway actresses, the Seventh Avenue designers, and the world's most famous rock star's most famous ex-wife, a woman to whom fame belonged like logic to a syllogism, axiomatically. Before the list was quite done, I caught a glimpse of something, a flash of saffron at the other end of the room, and I had to turn and look again.

Peering through a thicket of reed-necked women, I saw that I'd been right: yes, it was a monk in saffron robes, it really was a Buddhist monk—Tibetan, I was almost sure. He was sitting at the head of a table on the far side of the room, spectral in the glow of the restaurant's discreetly hidden lighting. But he was real. His robes were real robes; not drag, not a costume. He was in his early middle age, with clerically cropped hair and a pitted, wind-ravaged face. He happened to look up and happened to notice me staring at him. He looked surprised to see me: his chopsticks described a slow interrogative arc as they curled up to his mouth.

I was no less surprised to see him: he was probably a little less out of place among the dinner-jackets and designer diamonds than I, in my desert boots and sweater, but only marginally so.

He glanced at me again, and I looked quickly down at my plate. On it sat three dumplings decorated with slivers of vegetables. The dumplings looked oddly familiar, but I couldn't quite place them.

'Who were you looking at?' said the friend who'd taken me there, an American writer and actress who had spent a long time in India and, in gratitude to the subcontinent, had undertaken to show me the sights of New York.

I gestured foolishly with a lacquered chopstick.

She laughed. 'Well, of course,' she said. 'It's his show; he probably organized the whole thing. Didn't you know?'

I didn't know. All I'd been told was that this was the event of the week in New York, very possibly even the month (it wasn't a busy month): a benefit dinner in the Indo-Chine, the in-est restaurant in Manhattan—one which had in fact defied every canon of in-ism by being in for almost a whole year, and which therefore had to be seen now if at all, before the tourists from Alabama got to it. My scepticism about the in-ness of the event had been dispelled by the tide of papparazzi we'd had to breast on our way in.

Laughing at my astonishment, she said, 'Didn't I tell you? It's a benefit for the Tibetan cause.'

More astonished still, I said, 'Which Tibetan cause?'

'The Tibetan cause,' someone said vaguely, picking at a curl of something indeterminately vegetable that had been carved into a flower shape.

It was explained to me then that the benefit was being hosted by a celebrated Hollywood star; a young actor who, having risen to fame through his portrayal of the initiation rites of an American officer, had afterwards converted to Tibetan Buddhism and found so much fulfilment in it he was reported to have sworn that he would put Tibet on the world map, make it a household word in the US, like Maalox or Lysol.

'The odd thing is,' said my friend, 'that he really is very sincere about this: he really isn't like those radical chic cynics of the sixties and seventies. He's not an intellectual, and he probably doesn't know much about Tibet, but he wants to do what little he can. They have to raise money for their schools and so on, and the truth is that no one in New York is going to reach into their pockets unless they can sit at dinner with rock stars' ex-wives. It's not his fault. He's probably doing what they want him to do.'

I looked at the Tibetan monk again. He was being talked to by an improbably distinguished man in a dinner-jacket. He caught my eye, and nodded, smiling, as he bit into a dumpling.

Suddenly I remembered what the dumpling was. It was a Tibetan *mo-mo*, but stuffed with salmon and asparagus and such like instead of the usual bits of pork and fat. I sat back to marvel at the one dumpling left on my plate. It seemed a historic bit of food: one of the first genuine morsels of Tibetan *nouvelle cuisine*.

*T*he last time I'd eaten a *mo-mo* was as an undergraduate, in Delhi.
A community of Tibetan refugees had built shacks along the Grand Trunk Road, not far from the university. The shacks were fragile but tenacious, built out of bits of wood, tin and corrugated iron. During the monsoons they would cover the roofs with sheets of tarpaulin and plastic, and weigh them down with bricks and stones. Often the bricks would be washed away and the sheets of plastic would be left flapping in the wind like gigantic prayer-flags. Some of the refugees served *mo-mos*, noodles and *chhang*, the milky Tibetan rice beer, on tables they had knocked together out of discarded crates. Their food was very popular among the drivers who frequented that part of the Grand Trunk Road.

In the university, it was something of a ritual to go to these shacks after an examination. We would drink huge quantities of *chhang*—it was very dilute, so you had to drink jugs of it—and eat noodle soup and *mo-mos*. The *mo-mos* were very simple there: bits of gristle and meat wrapped and boiled in thick skins of flour. They tasted of very little until you dipped them into the red sauce that came with them.

The food was cooked and served by elderly Tibetans; the young people were usually away, working. Communicating with them wasn't easy for the older people rarely knew any but the most functional Hindi.

As we drank our jugs of *chhang*, a fog of mystery would descend on the windy, lamp-lit interiors of the shacks. We would look at the ruddy, weathered faces of the women as they filled our jugs out of the rusty oil-drums in which they brewed the beer, and try to imagine the journey they had made: from their chilly, thin-aired plateau 15,000 feet above sea-level, across the passes of the high Himalayas, down into that steamy slum, floating on a bog of refuse and oil-slicks on the outskirts of Delhi.

Everyone who went there got drunk. You couldn't help doing so—it was hard to be in the presence of so terrible a displacement.

It was an unlikely place, but Tibetans seem to have a talent for surviving on unlikely terrain. Ever since the Chinese invasion of Tibet, dozens of colonies of Tibetan refugees have sprung up all over India. Many of them run thriving businesses in woollen goods, often in the most unexpected places. In Trivandrum, near the southernmost tip of India, where the temperature rarely drops below eighty degrees Fahrenheit and people either wear the thinnest of cottons or go bare-bodied, there are a number of Tibetan stalls in the marketplace, all piled high with woollen scarves and sweaters. They always seem to have more customers than they can handle.

Once, going past the Jama Masjid in Delhi in a bus on a scorching June day, I noticed a Tibetan stall tucked in between the sugar-cane juice vendors. Two middle-aged women dressed in heavy Tibetan *bakus* were sitting in it, knitting. The stall was stacked with the usual brightly coloured woollen goods. The women were smiling cheerfully as they bargained with their customers in sign language and broken Hindi. A small crowd had gathered around them, as though in tribute to their courage and resilience.

I found myself looking around the restaurant, involuntarily, for another Indian face, someone who had been properly invited, unlike me. I suppose I was looking for some acknowledgement, not of a debt, but of a shared history, a gesture towards the buyers of those hundreds of sweaters in Trivandrum. I couldn't see any. (Later someone said they'd seen a woman in a sari, but they couldn't be sure; it might have been a Somali robe—this was, after all, New York.)

When I next caught the monk's eye, his smile seemed a little guilty: the hospitality of a poor nation must have seemed dispensable compared to the charity of a rich one. Or perhaps he was merely bewildered. It cannot be easy to celebrate the commodification of one's own suffering.

But I couldn't help feeling that if the lama, like the actor, really wanted to make Tibet a household word in the western world, he wasn't setting about it the right way. He'd probably have done better if he'd turned it into an acronym, like TriBeCa or ComSubPac. And sold the rights to it to a line of detergents or even perhaps a breakfast cereal.

TiBet (where the Cause is): doesn't sound too bad, marketable even.

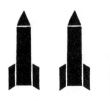

Notes on Contributors

Granta sent **Ian Jack** to Gibraltar shortly after the killings, where he spent six weeks researching his story. He has been a regular contributor to the London *Observer*, and is currently completing a book on India. His memoir of his father appeared in *Granta* 21. **Martin Amis**'s 'The Murderee' is from a work-in-progress that will be published next year. He is the author of five novels. His last book was a collection of stories, *Einstein's Monsters*. **Raymond Carver**'s writing has appeared in *Granta*s 4, 8, 12, 14 and 21. He first came to England in May 1986 at the invitation of the National Poetry Society. His forthcoming book of poems, *A New Path to the Waterfall*, was completed last June, shortly before he died. It will be published next year. **Tess Gallagher**'s first collection of stories is *Lover of Horses*, published last year. Her other work includes two collections of poems, *Instructions to the Double* and *Willingly*. This piece is an edited version of an address she gave at a memorial service for Raymond Carver, held on 22 September at St Peter's Church in New York. **Todd McEwen** is the author of one novel, *Fisher's Hornpipe*, and a number of stories, three of which have appeared in *Granta*. He has just finished a new novel and is currently living in Edinburgh. Of the seven town-centre pubs that **Graham Smith** began photographing in Middlesbrough in 1980, two have since been made into discothèques, three have been gutted and modernized—the Grand, for instance, is now called DeNiro's—and one has closed. 'The Pub' is his first published picture essay. **Nik Cohn** has written both the definitive history of Rock 'n' Roll, *Awopbopaloobopalapbamboom*, and the story that became *Saturday Night Fever*. He lives on Shelter Island in New York. His piece 'Immigrant' appeared in *Granta* 24. **Don DeLillo**'s most recent book, *Libra,* is based around the assassination of John F. Kennedy. He is the author of many novels, including *White Noise* and *The Numbers*. He was living in Greece at the time of the 1981 earthquake. **Angela Carter** has just returned from the United States. Her last book was *Nights at the Circus*. **John Berger**, art historian, essayist, poet and novelist, is a frequent contributor to *Granta*. *Once in Europa*, the second book of the fiction trilogy that began with *Pig Earth*, will be published next year by Granta Books. **John Sturrock** began his career taking photographs for *Socialist Worker*. His photographs of the British Miners' Strike of 1984–85 were published in *Blood, Sweat and Tears*. **Amitav Ghosh** has written two novels, *The Circle of Reason* and *The Shadow Lines*. His next book, the story of the time he spent living in rural Egypt, will be published in 1990 by Granta Books.